# THE FALKLANDS ASHTRAY

First published 2024

Copyright © Graham Logie 2024

The right of Graham Logie to be identified as the author of this work has been asserted in accordance with the Copyright, Designs & Patents Act 1988.

All rights reserved. No part of this book may be reproduced, stored in a retrieval system, or transmitted in any form or by any means, digital, electronic, electrostatic, magnetic tape, mechanical, photocopying, recording or otherwise, without the written permission of the copyright holder.

Published under licence by Brown Dog Books and
The Self-Publishing Partnership Ltd, 10b Greenway Farm, Bath Rd, Wick,
nr. Bath BS30 5RL, UK

www.selfpublishingpartnership.co.uk

ISBN printed book: 978-1-83952-851-4
ISBN e-book: 978-1-83952-852-1

Cover design by Kevin Rylands
Internal design by Andrew Easton

Printed and bound in the UK
This book is printed on FSC® certified paper

MIX
Paper | Supporting responsible forestry
FSC® C013604
www.fsc.org

# THE FALKLANDS ASHTRAY

A welder's experience at RAF Stanley – 1984

GRAHAM LOGIE

BROWN DOG BOOKS

Previous book by same author:
**Give Her Six**

# Endorsements

**Jim Davidson OBE** – Comedian and TV presenter – 'I love reading about my time in the Falkland Islands. The islands are beautiful and so are the people … all of them … honest! Enjoy Graham's book.'

**Richard Digance** – Comedian and folk singer – 'I flew 8,000 miles and performed to 8 British soldiers at San Carlos. It was my first ever sell-out concert! Good luck with the book.'

**Mrs Anya Bull (nee Smith)** – Falkland Islands resident – I am truly honoured to have been asked by Graham to write a few words for his book. It is rare to be able to read something about one's home and actually think 'This is all true, this is exactly what life was like during the first few years after the war'. Life was confusing, our home as we knew it was dirty, damaged and shell-shocked. Every aspect of our life had changed. As civilians we were still trying to make sense of what had happened to us two years before. Often you will read a book and end up angry because some things just aren't true. Graham's book is different. He has captured every detail and story with a refreshing honesty that brought back memories that had become hidden with age. I was a 17 year old nurse in Stanley in 1984 and the Falklands had been shaken to its core by the devastating hospital fire on April 10th. It has been a pleasure to write this and I hope you get the chance to visit the Islands again one day, to see how far we have come, to see the progress that has been made, and to see the incredible place our grandchildren get to call their home.

**Dave Gledhill** – Former Phantom Navigator and author of 'Fighters over the Falklands' – Having served in the Falkland Islands in the period soon after the end of the conflict, RAF Stanley was incomparable to other RAF stations. Beneath the façade of high tech weaponry, the hastily assembled base was a collection of ramshackle tents and buildings. Despite strict military discipline, in the background it had its own unique economy based on bartering. The author recounts fascinating stories of normal service life which was far from normal. What was life like both on and off duty? How did you get around the islands? How does a discarded shell case become a memento of life "Down South"? It's all here.

**Mark Harrisson FRAeS** – Ex Bristow helicopter pilot and currently Director, Greenair, Channel Islands - Graham's writing is engaging and, to those who were there, immensely precious as his recollection and detail so vividly bring to mind all we achieved together. The programme to recover Pucará and Huey aircraft, that filled my life so much beyond the flying that was my primary task, could never have happened without Graham's complete enthusiasm for my own questionable idea. I am forever in his debt. Lessons learned then are in everyday use now as I work to introduce Hydrogen-Electric Islander aircraft to the Channel Island passenger route. Graham, thank you for being there, for all you gave back then, and for making today's move to sustainable aviation possible.

•

This book is for:

My favourite niece **Helen Sinclair.**

Although I worked in the Falklands and Japan, and lived in the USA, I still think I come second in the family list of intrepid travellers after your recent excursions to the Far East and Australasia.
I'm very proud of you Helen.
(Okay, I know you're my only niece.)

And

**Steve** and **Jamie**, my son-in-law and grandson, who both followed me into the RAF. Jamie was posted to Mount Pleasant too.

# Contents

| | | |
|---|---|---|
| Introduction | | 11 |
| Chapter One | Setting the Scene | 21 |
| Chapter Two | Ascension to Stanley | 36 |
| Chapter Three | Working and Walking | 49 |
| Chapter Four | Coffins | 85 |
| Chapter Five | Entertainment | 96 |
| Chapter Six | Currencies | 105 |
| Chapter Seven | Flights | 119 |
| Chapter Eight | The Trailer | 134 |

# Introduction

Through my personal photographs and memories, I thought it would be a good idea to put pen to paper, or should I say, fingers to keyboard in today's terminology, to recall what it was like to live and work in the early to mid 1980s at the newly established RAF Stanley in the Falkland Islands.

The Falklands War in 1982 came as a surprise to a lot of us in the UK, not least because many of us hadn't a clue that the islands existed, where they were on the map, or that they were, in fact, British. However, through the daily press and television coverage, we couldn't help but be impressed with the scale and enthusiasm of the Task Force and then the subsequent coverage of the war itself. Although the war lasted only 74 days, images and place names are forever imprinted in our minds.

So, in my eyes, there are four periods in the Falkland Islands timeline in recent history about which people have varied levels of knowledge.

1. Pre-war, so anything before 1982, and there's a host of reference books about the islands' history, geography, farming, fishing and wildlife.
2. The Falklands War (April 1982–June 1982), multiple books are available where we can learn about battles, the Task Force, military equipment, heroic deeds, soldiers, transport, war poems, etc., etc, so many well-deserved recollections.
3. |RAF Stanley (1982–1985, after the war and before Mount Pleasant airfield opened), there are short informative features and quite a few photos available online if you use a search engine for specific dates and places.
4. Post-1985, the new Mount Pleasant Airport & RAF base had opened, providing a permanent British Forces presence, and a

new facility to allow wide bodied jets to land and revolutionise travel from Europe, and beyond, to the Falkland Islands. Also, there are many publications which celebrate and commemorate anniversaries of the War, such as 20, 30 and 40 years on, and how people and the islands have developed.

**Item 3** above is where I saw a gap in people's awareness of what the islands were like for a serviceman to live and work in, and when going through my photos I realised there was much to share. Our generation is dwindling and so stories should be recorded, firstly for younger generations to understand, and also for those having served at RAF Stanley and outlying posts at the time to reminisce. RAF Stanley existed for a short three or four years so it was a privilege, and certainly an experience, that not every serviceman got the chance to encounter. Living and working conditions were much more basic before I went there, and I dare say, improved a little after 1984, but hopefully I can give a meaningful view of the average days in the life of a serviceman, long before the Internet and social media changed our lives. Different trades and departments didn't mix a lot at work or socially so it would be nice to think that servicemen who were there around the same time will be interested to know how others lived and coped.

The idea of nowadays reaching the Falklands in one flight, with a refuelling stop, on wide-bodied jets using Mount Pleasant airfield, is appealing considering that the hastily assembled 127-ship Task Force (designated as Task Force No 317) in 1982 took 3 weeks from Portsmouth, and in 1984 we took nine days by aircraft and ship.

(Hastily assembled is probably an understatement for getting a Naval Task Force together. I shudder to think of the logistics involved, but I had sympathy with my uncle Ronald, serving in the Navy at HMS Nelson in

Portsmouth. Several Navy ships had just docked for the Easter break, and before some sailors had practically reached their own homes, Ronald was responsible for ensuring they were contacted with orders to return immediately as they were setting sail for the Falklands within days. His tales are legendary, of sailors thinking it was some kind of wind-up and in several cases, the Police were used to call at sailors' home addresses to convince them that they were to return immediately.)

Apart from being away from home for six months, with a young daughter at home, and swapping a Scottish summer for a winter only two and a half thousand miles from the South Pole, physically being in the Falklands was a great experience and I'm grateful for the opportunity, given that I felt I knew so much about the place with what I had heard and seen on TV. As I explain later, if I'd been away from home for six months and was based at Ascension Island, it would have felt like being short-changed as the Falkland Islands were the places we wanted to experience. A spell on Ascension Island would have been great for my suntan in comparison to the Falklands winter, but no thanks. One bonus as far as I'm concerned is that if you were posted to Ascension Island, that's what you experienced. If you were posted to the Falklands, you briefly experienced Ascension as well as lived on the Falkland Islands.

My book strives to tell of the hard work, long hours and ability to acclimatise to working in difficult conditions in temporary surroundings, while still enjoying the camaraderie and the opportunities to look around the islands. Really sunny days with bitingly cold winds were the norm but we were improving the working facilities every day whilst maintaining an efficient service for the aircraft squadrons, which is, after all, why we were there in the first place. Who would have thought that I'd be involved in part of the process of repatriating bodies back to the UK. I thought Medics, Church Ministers and Undertakers dealt with that kind of thing, so as a young welder, it came as a real surprise. That's certainly something that I didn't sign up for, but I found it humbling to be one of the last people on the islands to bid farewell to someone on their final flight home. There were entertainment shows laid on for us (Jim Davidson, Richard Digance, Tommy Vance and others), we got the chance to take plane and helicopter flights, and there were as many laughs as serious times at work.

It was just as interesting and intriguing to land on Ascension Island, albeit on fleeting stopovers on our way to and from the Falklands. News coverage was mostly about aircraft take-off and landings and didn't show nearly as much about Ascension and its landscapes. We just had an idea of its volcanic ash surfaces but it was an experience to see it first hand, even although we were only transferring to a different aircraft in both directions. And the intense heat was very welcome before, and most certainly after, a Falklands winter.

A stopover to refuel in Dakar, North Africa, on the way to Ascension was equally as memorable as it was in the dead of night, and we refuelled as far away from the terminal buildings as possible, surrounded by armed guards lurking on the edge of the floodlit area. I use the term 'armed guards' loosely, because despite their camouflage clothing and wearing berets, they looked like the most unmilitary bunch, with rifles slung over their shoulders and I didn't know whether to feel secure or threatened by their casual presence.

There are a couple of things I've found since I started writing, both with this and my previous book (titled *Give Her Six*). Firstly, copyright law, which I've found to be a combination of fascinating, extremely frustrating and quite frankly a hindrance to anyone genuinely wanting others to experience some very informative and nostalgic pictures. Sometimes it can take an eternity to find a particular photo, most often online, and it perfectly fits the subject I'm writing about, and sometimes it exceeds my expectations of finding something so relevant, and then I realised that I can't trace the owner of the picture or the photographer, and then it starts a chain of emails and messages to try every angle to get hold of the person that I need permission from. Frustratingly, even writing a book like this, or my inaugural book, which will hardly cover their publishing costs, they're classed as being 'for commercial gain', and therefore gaining permissions becomes that little bit more difficult and expensive. Unfortunately, knowingly using a photo which you are aware isn't yours, and stating that you tried your best to locate the owner of the photo isn't good enough in the eyes of the law if the rightful owner wants to challenge it. Luckily, in my first book, I couldn't believe the kindness of genuine people only too happy to give me permission to use their pictures, but there were a couple of photos that would have been of great interest to the targeted readership, but the author of the book they were in had died, the photographer was untraceable, and the consequences of using unauthorised material were just too risky.

Secondly though, and this is the good news story, with both books, I researched an awful lot of stuff on the Internet, and I'm blown away by the amount of interesting facts I've found out about things I was involved with, but I took them at face value at the time and never bothered to trace their origins or details. Until now.

For example, as you'll read, I flew into Wideawake Airfield in Ascension Island. It never dawned on me to think of where did such a crazy, romantic name come from. But I made a point of finding out and now realise it's to do with its proximity to a large permanent bird colony.

A venture I was involved in, was building a trailer to transport a captured Argentinian aircraft home to the UK. After building the trailer (and getting paid!), I didn't bother to find out if the mission was even successful. Recently, I discovered that the plane became a bit of a mystery because six abandoned Argentinian Pucará aircraft were claimed by the British Forces and thought to have been brought home to the UK, but the whereabouts of only five were known, and the one I was involved with, became known as the 'Missing Sixth British Pucará.' Through scouring the Internet forty years later, I discovered that the aircraft is still sitting in pieces in a couple of shipping containers, after making it to the UK, and subsequently sold on to someone in the USA.

The interesting acquisition and use of two ships, SS *Uganda* and MV *Keren*, to transport troops and supplies to the Falklands, completely passed me by. They were, to me, just two random vessels used by the Ministry of Defence during and after the war. Surely they were available and it was a simple job of completing some paperwork and hiring them, but no, when I researched them, each had a remarkable story about how they were bought or commandeered, and how they were rapidly (especially the SS *Uganda's* conversion to a hospital ship) prepared for service.

Some things within the book will resonate with servicemen who were stationed at RAF Stanley at the time, one of which was hill walking around the areas famous for the battles that happened there, Mount Tumbledown, Wireless Ridge, Mount Longdon etc. So many people wanted to go out walking on their day off each week, that the RAF encouraged it as an approved pastime and supervised and aided us. We were given packed lunches, transport to and from our intended starting point, radios, and maps and got help with planning routes. Everyone hoped they would stumble upon either a military item hidden in the long grass, or find somewhere that troops (British and Argentinian) in the war had made temporary shelters, that no-one else had come across. These outposts, or vantage points became fewer and fewer, and were virtually cleared by souvenir hunters by late 1984.

**The Falklands Ashtray** (surely nobody would possibly name a book after an ashtray!) was the most coveted souvenir to take home. Made from 105 mm diameter brass shell cases, I always formed them into ashtrays for anyone who asked, because I had the facilities in our workshop, but it was finding the spent shells in the hills that became the hardest part of obtaining such a souvenir. Needless to say they became much sought after bartering tools thanks to their rarity.

Flights around the islands were readily available if you knew who to ask and if you wanted to see more of the islands on your day off. Operators of helicopter flights with Bristows, as well as cargo and refuelling flights with RAF Hercules aircraft always ensured that any empty seats were offered to anyone keen to explore. However, sometimes you needed to get off your butt and go and ask for flights etc, because nothing came to you unless you put in a bit of effort.

Blueys (air mail letters), the wreck of the *Lady Elizabeth*, Coastels, Rubbs, Phantoms, Wokkas, freezing cold winds, transportation in the back of lorries, and unchilled canned beer, all bring back memories of a unique RAF camp and an experience we'll never forget.

Later in the book I'll talk about servicemen's stories, which are often meant to impress but you really have to sort the absolute facts from the exaggerations. One tale which ravaged through the camp was of people witnessing penguins being the best mine detectors, as they were blown sky high while traversing a beach. In reality it probably takes large breeds like the King and Emperor penguins to be heavy enough to activate a mine, so in their absence, the tinier breeds we were used to seeing probably didn't provide such a spectacle. But it's a great story if you're trying to impress newcomers on their first day. Similarly, I witnessed an online debate where people discussed if there were actually three

Coastel living accommodation modules at RAF Stanley, and not just two as first suggested by Parliament. Stories started coming out of the woodwork about redundant Coastels being towed out to sea and used as target practice for the Navy and RAF, before being destined for the seabed, while others convinced us that they were all towed away and made use of for further accommodation after Mount Pleasant airfield opened. (This was only 17 years after the oil tanker SS *Torrey Canyon* was famously bombed to disperse the wreck and crude oil spill after running aground off the Cornish coast, so perhaps some fantasies about the Coastels meeting the same fate were fresh in people's minds and were a bit exaggerated.)

Lastly, and something I don't mention in proceeding chapters, was one of the best quotes I ever heard from an RAF Officer while stationed in the Falklands. This officer was the Squadron Leader in charge of us, and one day he just had to vent his frustration.

I admit that, because it wasn't your run-of-the-mill RAF camp, and because we were often buried beneath layers of clothing, and because half the time we were walking with a parka hood covering our faces while battling wind and sleet, and because street lighting was non-existent, and because we thought we could get away with not following procedures to the letter, we were probably less than observant of our duty to salute or acknowledge officers when we met or passed them. So the Officer gathered everyone together and ranted on about how proud he was of his Queen's Commission, and told us he'd stand for the lack of discipline and respect no more. He indicated quite clearly that in the future, if we pass him in the street, we salute him. If we see him without him wearing his hat to return the salute, we still salute him. If we see him in the local shop, we salute him. Then his unforgettable quote: 'Even if you see me naked in the bloody bath, you salute me.'

That was it, about 30 assembled guys, all bursting a gut trying not to laugh out loud because he still had his serious face on. Firstly, the image was pretty hard to stomach, and also there should hopefully be no such chance encounter.

# Chapter One
# – Setting the scene

I don't think there's a single word I could write about the Falklands War (2$^{nd}$ April–14$^{th}$ June 1982) that hasn't already been penned. There are countless books recalling people's involvement in the war, how the war was won, how the islands were tactically reclaimed, the strategies behind individual battles, and equally as many books published on anniversaries 20, 25, 30 and 40 or more years after the hostilities ended, updating us on how the Islands and residents have recovered. You only have to Google 'Falklands War Book' and every subject is covered, from Falklands War Planes, Falklands War Logistics, Falklands War Poetry, Falklands War Diaries, Falklands War Battles, and Falklands War Heroes. And quite rightly so, as the war itself was so surreal and so unexpected and we rely totally on others to inform us of what it was really like to be there, literally in the firing line.

In November 2023, I was in my dentist's chair and discovered it's amazing how you'll talk about anything to distract from the pain you're about to endure. I think my reasoning, as a total coward, was that if I kept him talking he'd forget to do my teeth and send me on my way. He's between 30 and 40 years of age and I'd just presented him with a copy of my first book. I happened to mention that if I wrote another book, it would be about my time in RAF Stanley, less than two years after the end of the Falklands War. I was taken aback when his questions were, 'Who was that between then?' and, even more surprisingly, 'So who won?'

Forty-two years later, people in the UK of a certain age have probably forgotten so much about the war, but there's still many place names, people, ships and quotes that stick in our minds, and if they came up in a quiz question, we'd come up with the right answer to this day. *Sir Galahad*, Sir Rex Hunt, Goose Green, Mount Tumbledown, Ian McDonald, Malvinas, 'I counted them all out, and I counted them all back', to name but a few. Wars are like every other event, unfortunately, and when the press and television companies deem them no longer newsworthy, they disappear from our view, so only if you were around at the time and took a keen interest, would you be up to speed with the details.

For those not so well acquainted with the above names and phrases:
**RFA *Sir Galahad*,** was a Royal Fleet Auxiliary landing ship, famously bombed by Argentinian A-4 Skyhawk planes in Port Pleasant, Fitzroy.
Ex RAF pilot, **Sir Rex Hunt**, a British Government Diplomat, was the Governor of the Falkland Islands from 1980–1985, and who's official car was a very distinctive red London taxi.
**Goose Green** is a small, picturesque settlement in East Falkland, the site of a tactically vital airfield and infamous for the Battle of Goose Green on 28/29 May 1982, when the settlement was invaded and captured by Argentinian Forces, and the hundred or so residents imprisoned.
**Mount Tumbledown**, at 750 feet high, is one of the highest peaks on the western side of Port Stanley, with fabulous views over Stanley Harbour and Port William, and again famous for its battle.
**Ian S. McDonald**, christened The Voice of the Falklands War, was an MOD spokesman and was a familiar face conducting daily news bulletins on the television in the evenings during hostilities. Ian's no-nonsense, monotone delivery style, described by Secretary of State for Defence John Nott as dull, boring and brilliant, made him a trusted figure in the British public's eyes. Ian's emotionless delivery was intentional to, in his own words, 'lessen the impact of bad news'. If we recall the 5 pm briefings from the Prime Minister and medical experts during the 2020 Covid

outbreak, that's how focussed we were on Ian's report each evening.
**Malvinas** is the Argentinian name for what we know as the Falkland Islands.

And, '**I counted them all out, and I counted them all back**' was a memorable quote from a television news report by the late Brian Hanrahan onboard HMS *Hermes*, as reporting restrictions didn't allow him to identify how many Harrier jump jets had taken part in a mission against Argentinian Forces that day. Brian cleverly ensured that, despite Argentinian claims to the contrary, at least we knew that they were all safe.

The above are absolutely iconic names and phrases that spring to mind for anyone who was around at the time.

It's really quite remarkable how quickly we all became accustomed to the place names, considering the war only lasted less than 11 weeks, and prior to it starting, I admit, like many others, I hadn't the foggiest idea that the Falkland Islands even existed, let alone where they were on the map, and that they were British. But in the days before the Internet and the popularity of social media, the Press, the Government of the day, and the Television companies must take a lot of credit, because we were all very well informed of the activities during each day of the war. I suppose most of us, definitely myself included, wondered what on earth we wanted with islands off the southernmost tip of Argentina, and it also seemed bizarre that we owned a territory 8,000 miles away, and instead of being able to muster any surprise attacks, we sent an armada (the Task Force) of ships that would take three weeks to get there and we broadcast the triumphant send-off with hugs and flag-waving on terrestrial television for the world to see. This was a war like no other.

So, having served at RAF Stanley in 1984, two years after the war had ended, I take a lot of pride in telling others about what it was really like there, post-war. The airfield was operated for civilian flights pre-war and then, after hostilities ceased, it became an RAF station for four years until the permanent RAF Mount Pleasant airfield was built and operational. We saw countless hours of television footage during the war, but the whole scenario was surreal, and we could never get a feel for what the Falklands Islands were really like, let alone believe that we were witnessing a British Overseas Territory being invaded. Rather than feel aggrieved that I served a six-month unaccompanied tour in winter in the South Atlantic, I now appreciate the experience and am privileged to have seen the Islands and the remnants of some of the war's effects on them. I think I would have felt short-changed if I'd been posted to RAF Ascension Island for six months, as the Falklands were what we'd seen and heard most about on television, so this was a once-in-a-lifetime opportunity. It was nice to see Ascension Island en route, but it really was a stop-off point in both directions. A tour of six months in Ascension would have been sunshine all the way, and after six months in the Falklands we were weather-beaten wrecks, but the experience of being in the Falklands was actually worth it.

So the idea came about to relate in a book, along with personal photos, my experience of the life of a serviceman in RAF Stanley, two years after the war.

I was a welder in the Royal Air Force, stationed at RAF Lossiemouth, in Morayshire, in the north of Scotland. Taking the whole of the British Forces into consideration, not just the Royal Air Force, there were only two welders with aircraft welding qualifications stationed in the Falklands after the war. Aircraft welding qualifications meet the standards of the Civil Aviation Authority (and testing was thorough and frequent). Every operational RAF camp in the UK probably had between one and three aircraft welders, so the chances of me being 'selected' to go to the Falklands (that means you're going, Graham, and you've got no choice) were pretty slim, or so I thought. But I received my first notification in August 1983, when I was told of my requirement to serve a six-month tour of the Falkland Islands in May 1984. Also, and I found this to be fascinating military speak, as a requirement for the posting, in October 1983, I was to be 'awarded' an HGV III licence.

Roughly translated, that means go to RAF St Athan in South Wales (600 miles from home), pass a quick theory test, then drive round Cardiff in a Bedford TK lorry for three and a half weeks. This was a long time to be away from home, but at that time it was the RAF's policy to have one central driving school for everyone, regardless of where they were stationed. Actually it was the biggest skive I think I've had the pleasure of. No private firm would afford the luxury of one instructor and two pupils per lorry. Fortunately, our instructor, Mr Coward, was very partial to a cup of tea, so the routes were all impeccably planned and timed to include transport cafes mid-morning and mid-afternoon. So I spent 17 working days driving every morning, and being a passenger for the other pupil every afternoon. It was always an ambition to pass my HGV test sometime in my life and, hey presto, I'd just been handed a free opportunity, and passed my test first time. In fact, 10 years earlier I was never a great one for being ambitious. My father suggested that I follow him into distillery management, which wasn't for me at 19 years of age, so I walked past the RAF careers office in Union Street in Aberdeen, saw a picture of an RAF driver at the wheel of a lorry, thought 'that'll do for me', and went inside. Two hours later I emerged, having been persuaded inside that I had suitable qualifications to be an engineer, and the rest is history. So whether as a driver or an engineer, the RAF was always going to have paid for my HGV licence.

And so, in early May 1984, the journey began on a lovely sunny afternoon with a 5 pm train from Elgin to Aberdeen and onward to

Edinburgh, then picking up the sleeper train to Cheltenham. There, a bus was waiting to take us to RAF Brize Norton.

Actually, arriving by train before we got bussed to Brize Norton reminded me of my first day in the RAF in 1974, when we got off the train at Newark railway station to get bussed to nearby RAF Swinderby. You sit on a long train, thinking you're on your own, but when you alight from the train, and passengers rush off to their destinations, there's 20 short-haired lads all standing around the platform looking equally lost.

That day was spent getting kitted out and attending lots of informative talks and presentations on the Falklands and what was expected of us over the next six months. Of course, there were so many servicemen in the Falklands that we were like a peaceful invasion and tolerated rather than welcomed, so there were probably more presentations on what *not* to do, and who *not* to offend, than on what we could be seen to do. Considering there were a hundred of us, kitting us out ran pretty smoothly, although trying to organise us all must have been a bit like herding cats. This was still a kitting and posting procedure that was very much in its infancy, as serviceman in the RAF are normally posted individually, so getting us all, and our baggage, to a destination eight thousand miles away took a lot of organisation and was quite alien to us. It was quite unusual being in such a large group where no-one had any idea of what we were going to. Normally there's always someone who had been to a job or location previously and could tell us a bit about it. What also took me by surprise, and must have been a logistical nightmare, was hearing how many of the group were going to smaller outposts, radar stations and communications sites dotted all around the islands, like Byron Heights, Mount Kent, Ajax Bay etc., so getting to Port Stanley was just a stepping stone on their journey.

My last sleep was on a train, and the next night was going to be spent onboard a British Airways Lockheed Tristar aircraft, on temporary hire at the time to the Air Force, en route to RAF Ascension Island.

My lasting memory of the departures gate at Brize Norton was of a television news report of horrendous rioting between miners and Police during the 1984/5 miners' strike. This was to be significant six months later, because the first thing I saw on TV in Brize Norton on my return on 6th October, the day before my birthday, was an identical riot. As it happened, the strike lasted 12 months, but it was quite depressing to return and see no change in the six months I was away. With the lack of televisions in the Falklands, we probably didn't keep up with world affairs as much as we'd have liked.

The aircraft stopped briefly in Dakar in Senegal to refuel. We landed at about 2 am, and what I can remember is virtually total darkness as we came to a halt on a secluded concrete area at the far end of the runway, well away from any terminal building or other aircraft. We weren't allowed to disembark, and it just seemed quite unnerving, with little contact from the captain, but our simple instructions were to release our seat belts during the refuelling operation. As the aircraft door was to be opened to allow ground crew onboard, the cabin crew walked down the aisles liberally spraying and choking us all with aerosol cans of insect repellent. All we could make out in the moonlight and the headlights of a few vehicles pulling up beside the plane, was a small, very old and very overloaded fire engine, that wouldn't have looked out of place on TV's *Trumpton* children's programme, with the crew standing on foot plates and hanging onto the sides for dear life as it was travelling at speed. The 'firemen' were wearing T-shirts, shorts and wellies, hardly what you'd expect from people in readiness for a major aircraft blaze. In the partial moonlight, we could just make out silhouettes of what I presumed were soldiers, casually pacing around with rifles slung over their shoulders, forming a circle around us. Several of us commented that we weren't sure if they were protecting us from something (goodness knows what) or ensuring we didn't make a run for it (no chance). As quickly as the fire engine, 'soldiers', etc. appeared, the minute refuelling was completed, they all disappeared again into the darkness. This was a very quick, bizarre, uncomfortable stopover, certainly not very welcoming in any way, and none of us complained when we got the all clear to depart. The doors were closed and we promptly took off again, heading south, over the Equator.

Several hours later, and now in daylight, we approached Wideawake Airfield on Ascension Island, and it had the feeling of arriving at a normal holiday destination. Apart from having an RAF cabin crew, we were onboard a regular civilian airliner, the sun was shining, beautiful blue seas all around, everyone straining to see out the windows, excitedly getting a glimpse of a new destination for the first time. As the aircraft turned, and the wingtips lowered left then right, we, in the middle section of seats, could for the first time see fleeting glimpses of how barren the landscape looked, with the expanse of dark brown volcanic ash, not a patch of greenery in sight. Then the airfield came into sight and the array of planes, helicopters and equipment on the ground suddenly looked like an RAF airfield again and the 'holiday' feel disappeared. Everyone now desperately wanted to disembark. It had been a long night, we were tired, bored and hungry. Before anyone asks, I was as intrigued, as I assume you are, as to the origin of the name 'Wideawake Airfield'. The name is so bizarre that I don't think anyone could have hazarded a sensible guess and, as usual, I didn't think to ask then, but it now fascinates me. Adjacent to the airfield is a large permanent colony of Sooty Terns, locally nicknamed Wideawake Terns because of the constant (day & night) cawing chatter noises they make.

The airfield is also known more officially by the United States Space Force, who jointly share the facility, as Ascension Island Auxiliary Field, but Wideawake Airfield gives a far more romantic image. For a very small number of RAF guys on the plane, this was their final destination, but most of us were Falklands-bound, so some hurried 'Cheerios', and we went our separate ways.

There was no respite as soon as we left the aircraft. No fancy luggage carousel, just a disorderly case of grab your two kitbags from the two hundred or so identical bags on the tarmac as they were thrown (sorry, I mean unloaded carefully and speedily) from the hold, and then form orderly lines of ten soldiers/airmen, ready for the next leg of our journey. RAF Ascension Island had a real sense of, for want of a better word, busyness. There were several different types of aircraft on view, cargo and passenger planes and helicopters. The warm air smelled of aircraft fuel, various engines on the ground-support equipment for the aircraft were purring in the distance, helicopters hovered overhead, helicopter rotors were idling on the helipads, and voices everywhere were shouting directions and instructions. Thankfully it was a ridiculously warm, sunny morning, so the longer we were waiting in a queue, the better. The fresh air was very welcome, albeit a bit stifling with the lack of a breeze. I can't imagine people in Ascension say, 'Good morning, lovely day,' because it's always sunny (almost twice the hours of annual sunshine compared to London), so maybe they only comment if it's a rubbish day. Army personnel had also started flying in on several separate flights, so that explained the variety of passenger planes, and there was quite a crowd gathering now on the tarmac. At one stage during the Falklands War of 1982, Wideawake was declared the busiest airport in the world as far as the amount of aircraft movements were concerned. We knew the second half of our journey was by sea, and nobody was very forthcoming with information, but eventually it was our turn, and we were told to line up and wait for the next approaching Westland Wessex helicopter. Sure enough, long before we could see her, we heard the old bone-shaker above us. It turns out there were actually three helicopters running a shuttle service. We knew we were travelling the rest of the way by sea, but we were quite naïve and hadn't actually asked what ship the chopper was taking us to (incidentally, filling in a next of kin form for what turned out to be a five minute jaunt didn't exactly fill us with confidence). That really was the nature of the whole trip after getting off the sleeper train, following instructions and being shunted from one place to another like sheep. The helicopters' turnaround time was minimal, and after watching a couple of other groups boarding and taking off, nobody wanted to be the ones to hold anyone up. Quick instructions were shouted at us about keeping to marked pathways, keep clear of the tail rotors, throw your bags in, jump in and get seated. It was all really quite surreal, being whisked off the plane, trying to savour the atmosphere and believing we were actually in Ascension and Falklands-bound, and trying to take in everything going on around us. All was to be revealed as soon as we were airborne, because after only a couple of minutes into the flight, we could see, sitting below us, anchored in Southwest Bay at the end of the runway, was an old adversary of mine and our home for the next eight days – the SS *Uganda*.

Everyone recognised her from the television footage during the Falklands War two years previously, but I had also sailed onboard the *Uganda* in May 1971 on P&O's Schools Cruise No 235 to a not too dissimilar part of the world, namely Sao Miguel in The Azores and Funchal on the island of Madeira in the North Atlantic. Now the beautiful, white Passenger/Cruise ship I remember boarding 13 years previously in Greenock was a sorry looking, dirty, weather beaten hulk. In 1971 she was a clean, impressive vessel and the nearest we'd ever seen to a luxury cruise ship. This time she looked tiny, approaching her from the air, but in Greenock she was anchored offshore and we boarded her from a small tender, the *Uganda's* bright white hull towering above us in the early evening sunlight.

The SS *Uganda* had actually been commandeered by the British Government to serve as a hospital ship during the Falklands War. During a school trip in the Mediterranean on 10$^{th}$ April 1982, over three hundred regular passengers and nine hundred schoolchildren were hurriedly disembarked in Naples, and the ship, with Captain Brian Biddick in command, steamed to Gibraltar for an intense three-day refit. In those three days, fittings for replenishment at sea, satellite communications, wards and operating theatres were fitted, and she set sail for the South Atlantic with 136 medical staff aboard, including 40 members of the Queen Alexandra's Royal Naval Nursing Service. She looked absolutely resplendent, with a gleaming white structure and bright red crosses identifying her as a hospital ship, as we saw her on television joining the Task Force. Post-war, she was deregistered as a hospital ship and had her eight red crosses painted over. She was now in the middle of serving a two year stint as a troop ship. We landed on her helipad, which had also been hurriedly fitted in Gibraltar ready for war service, and made our way to the accommodation. I immediately got a flashback to 1971 when I was led through several passageways and entered the dormitory. Nothing had changed and we had a very basic bunk bed and a single locker each. On the school cruises, there was a master-at-arms who ensured discipline was maintained onboard. His favourite party piece was carried out at a ridiculously early hour every morning. He'd walk along the rows of dormitories, stick his head in the door of each one and, in his best Army Sergeant Major voice, he'd bellow, 'FEET ON THE DECK.' Believe me, we jumped out of bed. You could hear him three dormitories before ours, and you could hear his voice echo in the distance as he left and went from room to room. Woe betide anyone who was still in bed on his second circuit.

When I say that the vessel had been stripped of all the cruising luxuries since I'd last been onboard her, I am not exaggerating. Twenty sets of bunk beds to a dormitory, toilet facilities, a laundry, catering facilities, and that is that. What on earth were a hundred RAF servicemen and seven hundred Army personnel going to do in our new home for the next eight days – NOTHING.

Believe it or not, this is the second book I've written, and people assume that I must be an avid reader. Well, I had only read one book in my adult life between leaving Bowmore School on Islay in 1971 and, 50 years later, picking up my State Pension in 2021. And that book, *Kane and Abel*, written by Jeffrey Archer, was left on my dormitory bed, presumably by the occupant on the previous sailing. I admit, total boredom made me start reading it, but I absolutely couldn't put it down after that. I thought it might whet my appetite to read more books onboard, and maybe also when I was settled in the Falklands with nothing to do, but alas, it wasn't to be.

Once aboard, we were read the riot act immediately. Don't break anything, no running, no trouble, listen out for instructions and bulletins on the ship's tannoy, a maximum of two cans of beer per person could be purchased each day, no RAF/Army inter-service rivalry leading to fighting, and everyone will get along famously – WRONG.

We hadn't even sailed before one of the Army guys (affectionately known for the duration of the sailing as Grunts) decided to wash his size 10 boots in a washing machine, damaging the drum beyond repair, and all laundry facilities were immediately withdrawn. You couldn't write the script, could you. The message was clear, don't rock the boat (pun definitely intended) and we'll get along famously, but do one thing wrong and you spoil it for everyone. I suppose they wanted to get the message across by making an example of this poor guy.

Up on deck we were entertained by some of the ship's crew with their clever fishing technique. Casting long lines from one side of the ship, we watched the tension on the lines, eagerly awaiting a shout that there was a potential bite. The crew were fishing from about the third deck, so way above the water line. Any decent-sized fish would have been a bonus, but the elusive catch was the beautiful Mahi Mahi. When, eventually, there was a bite, their well rehearsed plan went into action. Unbeknown to us, the ship was an attraction for the scavenging, eat-anything, black trigger fish. Slightly different in size, and not as aggressive as a piranha, but a little nuisance, to say the least, to the fishers. So to reel in a Mahi Mahi through a shoal of triggers, would have resulted in a fish skeleton being landed. So, some resourceful crew members, stationed patiently on the other side of the ship, were given the shout to release a distraction. A whole tray of bread rolls and a bucket of food scraps were cast into the sea and, while the sea on the Port side was churning with trigger fish ripping the rolls to shreds, the crewman on the Starboard side successfully reeled in the untouched fish like a man possessed. Great entertainment in a beautiful setting, and a lovely leisure activity to break the monotony for the crew before another regular trip to the Falklands. The trip wasn't going to be a bundle of laughs for us, but I do sympathise with the unseen crew members in kitchens and engine rooms etc. who probably hardly ever see the light of day.

For a few minutes, it was easy to daydream as we stood against the railings of what was a one-time cruise ship, in our shirt sleeves, not a cloud in the sky, with the sun beating down on us, birds flying around the ship, and fish clearly visible below us in the crystal-clear water. Looking across the bay, Ascension Island looked magnificent. We'd been shunted off our plane, herded like sheep in the helicopter holding area, and boarded the helicopter relatively quickly, but now we had some time to take in our surroundings. Ascension is bizarrely quite beautiful, although predominantly made up of volcanic ash, with its highest point, The Peak, better known as Green Mountain, in the centre. The mountain has a permanent cloud around it and a completely different micro-climate at the top. We didn't see the top on our approach to the airfield, but were treated to a glimpse on the homeward journey, as I'll explain later. The airfield looked exactly as we'd seen on television as a bustling stopover point for everything in transit to the Falklands. A VC-10 passenger plane, four or five Hercules C-130s, three Tristars, a Nimrod, a couple of iconic Victor tankers, helicopters and every piece of available space littered with containers, portakabins and wooden crates. Our peace and quiet was to be interrupted time and again by the roar of the three thundering Wessex helicopters above our heads. Constantly running a shuttle service, ferrying airmen, soldiers and supplies aboard, there seemed to be one on the ship's helipad, one on the airfield and one in the air at all times, before we set sail for six months of winter in the unknown. Now I see why it was so important to board the helicopter efficiently, because any delay on the ground would have meant another helicopter queuing, and that would have disrupted a very efficient loading programme.

I was hoping that the ship might have made a rapid exit, and I was actually looking forward to the spectacle of us slowly getting under way as the helicopters made their final few cargo drops as we sailed, but everything was completed before the decision was made to go. Maybe the old Wessexs would have struggled to go too far out to sea if we'd sailed.

# Chapter Two
# – Ascension to Stanley

Getting this thirty-two-year-old veteran ship under way was quite impressive and exciting. The decks vibrated and the sea churned, and we did a 180 degree turn as her two massive engines pushed us up to speed, black smoke billowing from the *Uganda's* funnel, and people finding their way around, often running from side to side on the upper deck to get the best views and photos of Ascension Island as we turned out of the bay. It was quite comical, thinking about it now, but the first few hours spent on board a cruise ship are usually a great opportunity for guests to check out the entertainment, bars, restaurants, swimming pools and all the best seating and sun-lounging areas. Here, we now had 800 servicemen aimlessly roaming around the ship checking that indeed there was nothing on the first deck, nothing on the second deck, even less on the accommodation deck, etc, etc.

It was also quite surreal as we'd had such a hectic couple of days, and in no time at all Ascension was a speck on the horizon, and now we weren't to see land for a week. The *Uganda* felt quite impressive as we stood on the top decks, sitting at anchor in Southwest Bay, but all of a sudden she felt small and vulnerable as she started pitching through the waves in the open sea.

The beer quotas weren't available at some fancy bar, but were distributed from a couple of tables in an old lounge, and I think it was perhaps very naïve of us to have expected them to have been chilled. There were stacks and stacks of cans in original 24-can packaging; one brand of beer and one brand of lager. So no gins or cocktails on deck,

McEwans or Tennents, take it or leave it.

There was, of course the customary emergency drill at the muster stations, which was about the only time that everything went smoothly as everyone sensed a sort of duty to educate themselves on safety procedures, and one of the few times we saw all the RAF and Army NCOs and ship's officers all together at one time.

If ever there was a time to get to know people well, then sailing the Atlantic on an empty ship was a great opportunity. We knew we were heading for wintry weather, but the first two days of sunshine were there to be enjoyed, so we took advantage and spent countless hours on deck chatting. There was a guy, Gary, a Survival Equipment Fitter and neighbour of mine, who'd been with me from Elgin train station, and we had many chats on old fashioned deck chairs up on the top deck. A few brave, maybe foolish, souls or do-gooders tried their best at various times to set up some inter-service and inter-dormitory activities, mostly sport, fitness or quiz related, but they fell flat nearly every time and it was more entertaining watching the chaos and the arguments they caused than taking part. Predictably, with so many young men cooped up on a boat, there were a fair few serious keep fit enthusiasts and running round and round the deck, for what seemed like an eternity, kept them occupied. As for me, I've never voluntarily jogged on dry land in my life, and no way was I going to start doing it on a ship bouncing around in the southern Atlantic.

Highlights of the days were undoubtedly mealtimes and, before we even got to the galley, there was an event that infuriated, yet entertained the RAF contingent. We were in three adjoining dormitories closest to the food hall, and in an attempt to form orderly queues for serving meals, a voice would come over the tannoy announcing that meals were now available and the order in which dormitories were to proceed. The theory was to give everyone a chance at being first, and could and should have been a very fair way of doing things. It wasn't exactly rocket science and we, of course, waited our turn. So each batch of 40 guys would walk in single file in an orderly fashion when dormitories 1, 2 or 3 were summoned.

However, remember the thoughtlessness of the washing machine fiasco while at anchor? Well the Army guys knew that apart from dormitories 1, 2 and 3, every other dormitory was occupied by guardsmen. So for example, when dormitory 10 was first to be called forward, you may as well have shouted the word 'ARMY'. Pandemonium ensued. All seven hundred Army guys stormed the corridors, pushing and jostling each other. God help anyone trying to walk in the opposite direction in passageways only two persons wide. You can't buy entertainment like that, and we made sure we had a good vantage point each mealtime to watch the stampede. The vain attempts by the ship's crew and RAF and Army NCOs to maintain some sort of orderly queuing were futile but very watchable. Being last to go for meals was actually the most civilised time, plenty food to go round, seconds were always available, sit together with people you know, and a bit of peace and quiet.

Before the weather turned, we enjoyed a couple of evenings sitting outside on the upper decks, fascinated by the stars, and making the most of the last of the shirt-sleeve weather. Of course we also had to protect our rationed two cans of beer. Leave your seat unoccupied for a minute and they were gone. There were a few broken hearts when anyone tripped and spilled their last can, and just to rub salt in the wound, a rousing cheer would go up, just like back home when anyone breaks a glass in a bar or drops a plate in a restaurant. There was also a black market evolving, so if you didn't want to drink your allocation, there was always a willing customer wanting to buy it. Then, and probably not a great surprise to anyone, put eight hundred military guys together, bore them rigid on an empty troop ship, get them half drunk, and what do they do when they finish their beer, finish the black-market cans they either bought or bullied from people, and no-one will share any more with them? – *FIGHT*.

If nothing else, sleeping in 40-man dormitories certainly encouraged any joker in the pack to make themselves known. There's always someone wanting to be top dog. Picture the scene in our dormitory one night, all lights out and everyone finally exhausted and ready to sleep. It's midnight and a conversation starts between guys at opposite ends of the dormitory called Mitch, Barry and at that particular time, an unknown voice.

**Mitch** – 'Is there anyone here called Harry?'
**Unknown voice** – 'Yes, me.'
**Mitch** – 'Who's that?'
**Unknown voice** – 'Obviously Harry.'
**Mitch** – 'Hi Harry.'
**Harry** – 'Hi.'
**Mitch** – 'Harry, is your real name Harold?'
**Harry** – 'Yes.'
**Mitch** – 'BARRY !!'
**Barry** – 'Bloody hell, what.'
**Mitch** – 'Did you hear me talk to Harry?'
**Barry** – 'YES !!, I couldn't help hearing you.'
**Mitch** – 'Barry, is your real name Barold?'

There followed a deathly silence, then 40 blokes giggling uncontrollably like schoolboys. Other such occasions sometimes opened the floodgates and suddenly everyone was a comedian, but thankfully most evenings we slept, thanks to our two cans of beer. Actually, anyone without a sense of humour was going to have a pretty dull and lonely six months ahead. As you'll see in Chapter Four, humour was a way of getting through a very sensitive function expected of me as part of my job.

At 10 pm, all open decks were sealed off and the evening's clean-up would get under way. The tidy-up routine for the duration of the journey was that, each evening, six servicemen would be picked at random to pick up litter (mostly beer cans) and work in pairs on separate decks, supervised by a Ship's Junior Officer.

On the second evening I was chosen as one of the six. I've never won a raffle or the lottery in my life, but as soon as someone picks one guy out of 800 to pick up other people's rubbish, all of a sudden, my name is selected. As per instructions, the six of us were to go to the Ship's Bridge at a certain time, and be allocated our jobs from the Duty Officer. I hate being late for anything, so I was the first serviceman to arrive and was met by an extremely young Merchant Navy officer looking resplendent in his neatly pressed, white uniform.

We got chatting, and I told him I lived in Royal Air Force married quarters in Elgin, in Morayshire, and I was surprised when he told me that his family roots were in Forres, 10 miles away. It seemed an eternity before the other five 'volunteers' arrived, so we had a chance to continue our conversation. Next, I mentioned that my Dad worked in the whisky business all his life and, coincidentally, the officer's Grandad did too. Then I said that Dad started as a stoker in Benromach Distillery in Forres, and of course, again, the officer said that his Grandad worked at the same distillery, at the same time. So we exchanged family names and I said I would certainly check to see if my family remembered the names from what was probably 40 years previously. Sure enough, when I wrote to my parents, Mum said that Dad and the guy's Grandad were great friends and work colleagues for years and our families still exchanged Christmas cards for many years after we moved away.

Now, I'm fascinated by coincidences. That was the only night both myself and the officer were on litter-picking duties. By chance we both got there early and we had time to chat, both of us were stuck on a ship in the South Atlantic, and both closely related to old workmates in a tiny Scottish Distillery in the 1940s.

The days onboard were long. Apart from reading my book, or walking aimlessly round and round open decks and chatting, there certainly wasn't a lot of thought that went into occupying or entertaining eight hundred blokes for eight days.

One thing I did notice was that great friendships were established due to spending so much time together. Probably every RAF camp in the UK had at least one serviceman amongst the 100 of us, so we'd descended on Brize Norton literally from all over the country and most of us had met for the first time. Later on, when we worked at RAF Stanley, when you went to the Mess for a meal, you were equally as likely to look out for someone you had spent eight days with on a ship to sit beside, as someone you worked with for five months.

Days into the trip, the weather steadily worsened. It was lovely spending days outside when we could, watching albatrosses sweeping over the waves against a background of dark, cloudy skies. Albatrosses (yes, that's the plural) use soaring techniques to conserve energy, can create lift from the wind rising over high waves and are remarkably graceful considering their two to three metre wingspans. Their wingtips looked to be just inches from the water as they swooped left, then right, almost as if putting on a show for us. Unfortunately we never got to appreciate the exact size of the birds as they always kept cautiously distant from us. I don't think we saw another single ship throughout the trip as we were literally in the centre of the South Atlantic, as far as possible from land in every direction, and it was fascinating wondering where a tired albatross would land. (Apparently, from the internet again, they can land on water and live, eat and sleep at sea for years. Every day's a school day.)

One night I vividly remember, probably about five days out, we hit particularly heavy seas. I woke up to the thunder of locker doors banging and suitcases flying across the dormitory, and I swear, I thought the ship stood on her stern. Maybe it wasn't quite as dramatic as that, but feeling her being tossed around immediately after waking up scared me. After all, the scariest boats I'd been on previously were MacBraynes and Western Ferries car ferries to and from the Island of Islay in Argyllshire, and the Ballachulish ferry. The flat bottomed MV *Lochiel* used to frighten me as a boy as she rolled in heavy seas in the early 1960s, between Islay and the mainland, and at Ballachulish, before the bridge was built, the six-car ferry deck was a turntable and our car would be suspended above the water as the deck was spun 180 degrees, but this particular night was a whole new level. Next morning, after breakfast, yes it takes a lot to put me off my food, we went to the stern of the ship as she was still pitching heavily. Doors to the outside decks were locked, so the best entertainment was sitting on the semicircle of seats that bent around the stern windows. As the bow rose majestically, the stern ploughed into the waves and the windows were right on the water line. Then the bow would plunge deep into a wave and, as the stern rose, the propeller almost came out of the water and there was a tremendous vibration below our seats.

One thing I was completely delighted about was that I went to the Falklands on that particular week, and it was SS *Uganda* on the troop run. Had it been a week or so earlier or later, I'd have been onboard the second of the two Troop Ships, MV *Keren*.

She started her life as MV *St Edmund*, a Sealink cross Channel ferry, and was requisitioned by the Government to join the Task Force to ferry troops for active service. She was then subjected to compulsory purchase by the British Government in 1983 to act as a troop carrier. Her name change was interesting because when she was bought over, her crew, who were members of the National Union of Seamen (NUS), disputed whether they should receive their normal 'ferry' pay rate, dictated by their old routes, or a 'deep sea' pay rate, in anticipation of sailing in the South Atlantic. They went on strike and, as there was urgency in getting her onto the troop runs from Ascension Island to the Falkland Islands, a plot was hatched by the MoD to commission her as a Navy vessel and sail her with a Royal Navy crew. Thirty-five Royal Navy sailors boarded her and, once the Commissioning Warrant was read out, it became an offence for any members of the public to board, in this case specifically the NUS strikers, and sentries were posted on the gangways to allow only authorised personnel to 'take over' the ship. On receiving her commissioning, she was rechristened HMS *Keren*. The pay dispute was short-lived following the Navy's successful eight-day familiarisation and sea trials in the North Sea and, before she set sail, her original crew returned to work, having realised that the strike was futile because the Navy could successfully operate the ship without them. Her short-term commission was subsequently removed, but she kept her new name and became known as MV *Keren*.

Having been built originally just for cross Channel operation, she was more flat-bottomed than the SS *Uganda* and bounced around like a cork in the South Atlantic's unforgiving seas. This keel issue (or lack of a decent keel issue) became more apparent if the winds got up when she tried to enter Stanley Harbour. Often she'd have to sit at anchor outside the harbour for one or two days because if she'd tried manoeuvring through The Narrows, towards the pier at Port Stanley, the strong crosswinds would have blown her onto the rocks. So after an eight-day 'cruise' from

Ascension, passengers would often have to endure another one or two days onboard, waiting for the winds to subside. I never actually spoke to anyone who sailed on her, and maybe there was more to do onboard her compared to the SS *Uganda*, but for seaworthiness I was happy with our ship.

One memory I have of our approach to the Falklands, was that the landscape and scenery could have been any island off the West coast of Scotland. The similarities were quite surprising, considering we were well over 8,000 miles from Scotland. Luckily our approach was slow as daylight broke and we kept relatively close to the northeast coast of East Falkland, so we got some terrific views, and it was so reassuring to see land again.

And so, eventually, our eight-day trip was over and the harsh reality of why we were there dawned on us. It was a beautiful, calm, sunny morning as we inched into Port William Sound and then made a tight left-hand turn round the natural rocks forming The Narrows, the perfect entrance and shelter for Stanley Harbour. Our first impression was of lots of white buildings and houses with brightly coloured roofs (greens, blues, reds and terracottas) in Port Stanley, and although the sun was low in the sky, the drop in temperature from what we'd left in the UK was very evident. It appeared to be a reasonably busy harbour and there seemed to be helicopters scurrying about in all directions. It was almost like a mini episode of the TV programme *M\*A\*S\*H*, where every outdoor scene always seemed to have a chopper overhead. Coincidentally, the SS *Uganda*, in deference to the TV series *M\*A\*S\*H*, was nicknamed N.O.S.H. (Naval Ocean-going Surgical Hospital) by her crew during active war service. Her very apt call sign, considering the care she gave to injured British (580) and Argentinian (150) servicemen, was Mother Hen.

On disembarking, it was actually a helicopter that provided the first 'incident'; or maybe 'spectacle' is a better description. As we stood waiting for transport (the area, the RAF camp and the roads weren't suitable for buses yet, so any large numbers of passengers were ferried in the back of camouflaged Bedford lorries), a military Chinook helicopter roared over the bay and, importantly, well clear of any shipping below. Just as well, because we joked with each other that we'd been treated to a welcoming fly-past, but this in fact turned into quite a spectacular incident. The helicopter had two cargo nets slung below her, containing what looked like wooden boxes. The forward load started swinging from side to side and would probably have caused quite a handling problem, so the aircraft, rather than ditch the load in the sea, seemed to divert (I don't know where her destination was) to the closest clear landing area near Windy Ridge to stabilise the load.

Home for the next five to six months was to be a three-man room in Coastel 1. Coastels are basically floating versions of accommodation modules, similar to those on oil rigs, capable of housing 930 people. They must have been a welcome improvement for guys accommodated in tents or on ships at RAF Stanley after the war. We were basically custodians of RAF Stanley for the interim period of June 1982 to May 1985, until the permanent Mount Pleasant airfield was completed, so Coastels that arrived in early 1983 filled the accommodation void nicely and with relative comfort. As you can see from the Parliamentary questions below, redundant cruise liners were suggested as accommodation before the Coastels were established.

The following extract is from the House of Lords sitting on 20th December 1982:

**Lord Balfour of Inchrye** – My Lords ….. to ask Her Majesty's Government what is the approximate length of time that Royal Air Force and Army personnel are expected to serve in the Falkland Islands before return posting to the United Kingdom.

Further, may I ask ... for how much longer will men be under canvas during the bitter, winter conditions?

Are prefabricated buildings being exported from this country to the Falklands?

Is there any possibility of laid-up liners being used, since at present there are great numbers in our harbours and estuaries on the South coast?

**Viscount Long** – My Lords, British troops serve a five-month tour in the Falklands.

Last week, the first of the hotels, called the 'Coastel', arrived off Port Stanley. It will house 930 men. It has been decided to lease hotels of similar size to be in position in April 1983; that is, there are to be two.

Prime Minister **Margaret Thatcher,** when asked to update on the welfare of armed forces personnel serving in the Falklands, announced in the House of Commons on 28th June 1983:

'.... Two Coastels are now in position in the Falkland Islands...... A third Coastel is planned which will provide a further squash court and gymnasium ...... Educational facilities are available, as are some indoor entertainment facilities, and personnel also have a free postal service to the United Kingdom ... The standard tour length has also been reduced so that personnel, with very few exceptions, posted to the Falkland Islands serve only five months including time in transit.'

Having read that now, and not seen it 40 years ago, I'm quite comforted that our accommodation and welfare were given fairly prioritised attention, and, regardless of our opinions of the House of Lords, sitting 5 days before Christmas was surprising and admirable. Obviously there was going to be a transition time between the end of hostilities and a permanent base at Mount Pleasant, but it was important to move away from tented accommodation and bring a bit of peacetime comforts for those serving there.

*A tired looking SS* Uganda.

*Coastels 1 (closest) 2 & 3, taken from Navy Wasp helicopter.*

The Coastels were berthed on the shoreline, with a typical ship's gangway to access them, on the edge of RAF Stanley, just over a mile from the town. Coastel 1 had reasonably spacious, three-man rooms, with a single bed and a set of bunkbeds in each, and with good lockers/wardrobes. You could tell they'd been designed as worker's accommodation for the oil and gas industry, where large numbers of people would be starting and stopping shifts at the same time. There was a very high ratio of toilet and showering facilities per head, which did make our lives reasonably comfortable.

Officially described as shallow draught non-propelled vessels, the three Coastels were all owned by various companies, governments, etc. over the years and, accordingly, were renamed by each owner, up to seven or eight different times in their lifespan. In 1984, during their British Forces contract, they were named Safe Dominia, Pursuviant & Safe Esperia (thank goodness someone had decided that Nos 1, 2 and 3 would be easier for us simple servicemen to remember).

The Coastels had their own desalination plant, electricity generating plant, canteen, gymnasium and laundry facilities, so were quite self sufficient. There was also a bar outside Coastel 1 (unimaginatively called 'The Shed'), set up in a portakabin adjacent to our Coastel entrance, so pretty much everything we needed was on our doorstep.

# Chapter Three
# – Working and Walking

Day one, as I mentioned earlier, started off cold but brilliantly bright, with the sun low in the sky over RAF Stanley as we slowly glided into Stanley Harbour. It was a bit shambolic with everyone wanting off the ship, trying to keep our luggage handy, yet trying to get first glances and photos of an unusually colourful town.

There certainly was 'no rest for the wicked' once we'd disembarked. RAF guys off first, packed like sardines onboard a lorry, we got a rude awakening to the condition of the roads. Having been brought up on a small island and worked on my brother-in-law's farm, I was pretty used to hanging on and keeping my balance in the back of various vehicles on bumpy tracks and roads. It took about 20 minutes to get to the Coastel. Again, as per most of our travel arrangements, we had no clue what we were letting ourselves in for as far as our accommodation was concerned. None of us had ever seen or heard of one of these modules, but it sounded a bit like 'hotel', so fingers crossed. In no time at all, we got our belongings and our bedding up into our rooms, filled in some paperwork, as was customary for everything in the Services, then into the truck waiting outside to take us to the camp for the first time, where we were expected to make ourselves known and available to our places of work. Reality kicked in when we drove past the eerie sight of wrecked Argentinian aircraft on rough ground within the camp boundaries.

Transport was always going to be in the back of a lorry, to and from work. Surprisingly, there were some brand new vehicles out there, but there was also a fair splattering of things destined for the scrap heap. Luxury travel could be described as a lorry with a canvas-covered trailer, with wooden slatted seats along both sides and plenty of leg room. Working class was the same, but also included two additional rows of slatted seats back to back in the centre of the trailer, so I'd describe the cramped leg room as that of a very cheap airline. Economy was a covered trailer, no seats, and a couple of dangling ropes to hang on to for dear life. In fairness, the non-seated versions were few and far between, but it was a gamble as to what vehicle appeared each time. RAF Stanley roads had potholes like no other, so some drivers carried on straight over them, while others weaved from side to side like David Coulthard on a warm-up lap. Either way, it was every man for himself in the back, a bit like the big buses you get to transfer you from the terminal to the planes at foreign airports where you have to be onboard early to find a good holding point, otherwise you're just kept upright by the bodies packed around you. We often joked in the back that, judging by the speeds and the heavy braking, we were pretty sure that some of the less worldly-wise younger drivers forgot that it was a live human cargo they were transporting. Either that or they had a devilish sense of humour or a damn sadistic streak in them. The good thing about the canvas canopy over the trailer was that you could bang your fist on the roof of the cab to vent your displeasure if the ride got too uncomfortable.

Work for me was in the Station Workshop, a large, temporary, tented building made by Rubb. Rubb, a specialist PVC tent provider from the North-east of England, manufactured various tented, temporary buildings, specialising in aircraft hangars, typically sized to comfortably house one fighter jet per tent with working area around it, and the one we occupied was exactly that size. RAF Stanley was a hurriedly expanded camp, built and vastly extended on the site of a small, existing civilian airfield, and was mainly made up of such tents as well as portakabins and shipping containers. Not only did our Rubb accommodate our workshop machinery, benches and office, the rear half was also occupied by two RAF carpenters with all their equipment (planer/thicknesses and bandsaw) and wood storage. In one corner we had a 20 ft shipping container, converted into a machine shop, holding all of our electrical equipment, centre lathe, grindstones and pillar drills. There was also a very small corner of our half of the Rubb partitioned off, and it housed one of the aircraft trades, probably some sort of electrical bay if my memory serves me well. One thing I do remember is that whoever was in that bay had a cassette player permanently switched on and played Billy Joel's *Innocent Man* album constantly. I suppose consideration had to be given to it being a 'field' workshop facility, as nothing was permanent at this stage, and it was relatively soon after the war, but thinking about it now, putting naked flame welding equipment, gas cylinders, dust-producing woodwork machinery, bundles of horsehair padding and a stock of wood inside a rubber tent, could be risk assessed as quite a fire hazard in today's Health-and-Safety-conscious world.

So there were a couple of reasons I was chosen to go to the Falklands, and specifically why I got my HGV licence. Firstly, the type of aircraft stationed at RAF Stanley was the McDonnell Douglas F4 Phantom FGR2. Previous to me going to the Falklands, I had had four years' experience, not of physically working on Phantoms as much as Airframe trades, but of specifically welding one particular component in situ on the planes when I was stationed at RAF Wattisham in Suffolk (1977–80).

Along the front leading edge of each wing, and similarly along the rear trailing edges of the wings, there was a stainless-steel air duct and regularly (one incident per fortnight on a station where Phantoms were based, wasn't uncommon) a small crack, maybe only a quarter of an inch (6 mm) would appear. Normal protocol for any similar issue or fault on an aircraft part would have meant its removal and replacement or repair in a workshop. However, such removal of these particular components was labour intensive to say the least. A typical removal, repair and replacement could have taken a minimum of 24 hours and involved 3 or 4 technicians.

I once carried out what I jokingly called the two most expensive welds in RAF history. Our RAF Wattisham Phantoms were temporarily based at RAF Wethersfield during Wattisham's runway resurfacing in 1977. I lived in married quarters at the old HMS Ganges in Shotley Gate, 50 miles from Wethersfield. Two days in a row I travelled from home to Wethersfield and carried out a quarter-inch weld. So, two days work, two hundred miles driving in total, to weld half an inch of stainless steel.

Thankfully a technique was developed whereby we could weld these components in place on the aircraft in less than an hour, so the extra availability of a serviceable aircraft, and the reduced repair turnaround time, were a huge bonus to the squadrons. There was no official training for such a job, which is very unusual in aircraft repairs. I was never shown if it appeared in any aircraft repair manuals, no exams to pass and, understandably, no spare Phantoms you could practice on, but the knack of carrying out this delicate repair was handed down from welder to welder as we came and went from RAF Phantom stations. I have my great friend Dave Askew to thank for patiently teaching me. I hope Don Muirden went on to greater things after benefitting from my words of wisdom before I left Wattisham.

The job wasn't without risk, but was well managed, and for workshop-based fitters like myself, was a great experience to get up close to the aircraft. The first difference I noticed working in RAF Stanley, was transporting the welding plant to the planes. It had to be towed as it's so heavy and it had the tiniest wheels. So, after being used to near-perfect roads and airfields in the UK, this thing, packed with delicate electronics, now had to bounce along a bumpy dirt track. Now, the wing of an F4 Phantom is a bloody big fuel tank, so how did it make sense to weld something adjacent to it. The fuel tanks were actually filled to capacity before the welding took place, as the gases in an empty tank are more dangerous than the liquid in a full tank. The Phantom wings were a perfect height for working on, and the cracks were always at eye level, so very easy to stand firmly when welding such a thin piece of metal. The argon-arc (TIG) welding plant required the use of a foot pedal, similar to a car accelerator, to operate and regulate the electrical power, so working on a stable floor was essential. The rules were that the procedure was to be undertaken just inside a hangar, with the end doors open, and no-one else working on the aircraft. A tractor, with engine running, had to be coupled up ready to tow the plane away should anything go wrong. A competent person had to sit in the cockpit ready to release the brakes, and an engineering officer had to oversee the whole job. A fire engine also had to be in attendance. With all the safety procedures in place, everything went well 100 per cent of the time.

All work had to stop on the aircraft while the actual weld was carried out, so a small, interested group typically gathered around you. It was a bit nerve wracking because it was such a delicate job. The sense of achievement and relief when it was completed was immense. After we filed down the weld to allow the metal surfaces on the duct to slide smoothly over and under each other, a crew chief had the last word as to whether it was acceptable. I used to liken it to the tinned fruit advert when everyone stood quietly in anticipation, until the man from Del Monte, he say ... 'Yes.'

I had the distinction of being the only welder to have welded a duct on aircraft XV424 when she was painted in the stunning livery in 1979 in commemoration of Alcock & Brown's first transatlantic flight. Of course, on that occasion, she flew in to RAF Wattisham at night under cover of darkness and, on inspection, was found to have developed a crack on a duct. In typical 1970s RAF health & safety non-conformance, this weld was to be done in secrecy next morning before the official unveiling. So, in complete contrast to every precaution we'd normally adhere to, it was to be hangar doors closed, no tractor coupled up to the aircraft, no bright red fire engine to attract attention, just get on with it and to hell with the rules. Normally I'd make a fuss at other people's disregard for following procedure, but, instead of the nearest available junior officer being lumbered with supervising the task, a very fidgety Wing Commander was in charge that day, and his brief was that if photos of this stunningly painted aircraft were leaked before the Press release, heads would roll, so I took the easy option and just did the job. (To be honest, being ordered not to follow rules is quite satisfying really, and gives you a bit of leverage next time someone pulls you up for something.)

Jokingly, when welding the leading (front) edge of the wing, the more experienced engineering officers would just let you get on with it, probably a case of 'If I don't see a problem, there is no problem,' but if a brand new really young looking engineering officer was put in charge, I used to tease them before we started and ask why everything was being put in place to tow a potential blazing inferno out of the hangar if it went up in flames, but the poor guy doing the welding had to stand in front of the plane. I said in the event of a fire, my options for a quick death were to burn or get run over. Once I saw the blood drain from their faces at the prospect of having to make a decision, I reassured them I'd run away like a rat up a drain if I ever saw danger.

So there were only two of us RAF aircraft welders supporting the Navy, RAF and Army at any time in the Falklands, and it made sense for us to have experience of welding Phantoms. And, of course, my boss, the other qualified welder, wasn't going to come out of his snug office on a South

*Station Workshop Rubb tent (left)*

*23 Squadron Phantoms*

Atlantic winter's morning to do such a job, so I got all of them to do.

The reason I got my HGV licence, was that we worked in adjoining Rubbs to the aircraft ground support equipment trades (GSE), so they regularly needed the help of HIAB lifting equipment, which was mounted on lorries. The equipment they worked on had heavy engine covers, and this was the easiest way to lift them off to expose the engines for servicing. Although Rubb tents were robust, they were still only coverings, so unlike any workshop facilities back home, there was nowhere to hang overhead hoists (unless very specialist tents were used), but ours were just walls and a roof.

(Since I've decided to research everything for the book, I looked up HIAB. It's a word I've used throughout my working life and never questioned the acronym. It's short for the Swedish company that invented it – Hydrauliska Industri AB. Now there's a piece of information I'll never need again in my life.)

So, bear with me, I'm still on day one. It was beautiful and sunny and calm in the morning, and I've now introduced myself to my new workplace.

You've heard the saying about seeing all four seasons in one day. This was such a regular occurrence in the Falklands. When my bosses and I went through all our formal introductions and a few housekeeping rules, they said that there was no time like the present, I could start straight away, and could I go and sign out a lorry with a HIAB, as they had a job for me. By this time, the cold, sharp, sunny weather had been taken over by clouds, hail and snow.

I got the lorry as requested, and before I tell all about it I apologise to all environmentalists reading this for not being very responsible. I was told to load three 45-gallon drums of old engine oil, and that was all I needed to know. Unfortunately, and it will become clear in a minute as to why it was an issue, the hazardous contents signage on the drums had no relevance to the new contents. A couple of servicemen with more local knowledge than me would come with me to show me where to dump them. Unfortunately, 'dump' them was exactly the final outcome and maybe 'be sure to place them somewhere you are sure is safe, Graham' would have been a better choice of instruction. I hadn't the foggiest idea of my bearings, but I dutifully loaded the drums with the HIAB and tied them securely. Two guys jumped into the cab with me and assured me of their experience and length of service at RAF Stanley, and that all I had to do was follow their directions. I think that was meant to be reassuring. Of course, it was now early evening, dark and snowing. Snowing hard. Hard enough to cover vehicle tracks, and everything was a white blanket. We didn't finish work till 7 pm so we decided to still go ahead with the job. I followed their instructions and it seemed to make sense, out of the airfield, past the Coastel, along the main road towards Port Stanley, and turn right. Turn right into what? I don't know. Anyway, after sliding about in the snow, the guys with me said things like, 'I'm sure it's around here,' and, 'Who cares if it's not exactly right,' then suddenly, 'Stop here, this is where they go.'

Obviously I now realise that it was dinner time, so time was critical, and we were all cold and hungry. They just knew that there was a concreted area where waste 'could' be stored, and it was 'vaguely' somewhere near here. We offloaded the three drums, left them on their sides, and again my reassuring new colleagues said they would come back and store them neatly the next day. Somehow we negotiated what I believed to be a track, found the main road and made our way back to camp. I was happy that I'd helped on day one. They were happy that I was the driver and that they'd conned me to place the drums anywhere and get home. So, plenty to occupy me on my first night. Locate the Mess, have dinner, and find out where to catch the lorry back to the Coastel. I unpacked all my belongings properly and then had a well-earned sleep after all the settling in and the very fresh air.

Jumping swiftly to day two, the snow had all but completely gone and it was very cold. I got to the workshop at 7 am and was told, 'Logie, you're going to be a busy guy around here since we haven't had a driver for a while. Go and get another lorry, drive to the other side of Port Stanley and pick up some materials.' Again, someone with more local knowledge would come with me. With hindsight, I think I'd now prefer someone with common sense, and not these characters with 'local knowledge', to assist me.

I was getting the hang of this now. Out of the airfield, past the Coastel and along the main road to Port Stanley. Now, there was never usually enough vehicles to cause a traffic jam, but today, a few hundred yards towards Port Stanley, traffic was slowed down to single file because there were police Land Rovers and a couple of lorries parked on the verge on the right-hand side of the road. Each vehicle was flagged to slow down and was approached by a military policeman telling everyone that there had been an incident and to be cautious passing the parked vehicles because some idiot had dumped three full, unmarked drums of an unknown liquid on waste ground at the roadside last night. I think I muttered something like, 'That's unbelievable.' Well there was no way I was taking the blame for that one, so I buttered the policeman up a bit and asked him if I could be of assistance. He declined and thanked me, stating that moving along was the best thing I could do. If only he'd known that me not having been so gullible the previous evening would have been the best thing I could do!

At the beginning of the paragraph I apologised to environmentalists for 'not being very responsible'. Perhaps 'being totally irresponsible and being economical with the truth to a policeman' was a better turn of phrase.

For those of us with a sense of humour it was quite comical, with the snow melted, seeing the three random drums with a hazardous tape cordon around them, literally sitting in no man's land.

Throughout my time there, lots of opportunities arose to go out for a spin in a lorry, which I never turned down. There was an official refuse tip on the road to Moody Brook on the other side of Port Stanley from the airfield, so there was always someone requesting my services to take a load of rubbish there. In fact it didn't have to be a load, just a few bits was a reasonable enough excuse for a jaunt. And, of course, no-one had a clue how long it should take, so it was right up my street as I hate being timed. It was always good to stop and have a chat with someone, which I put down to befriending the local community, or maybe taking a teeny-weeny detour on the way back, which I regarded as acclimatising myself to the area. I had loads of excuses ready, just in case anyone questioned my timekeeping – The refuse tip was late opening, Traffic in the town was slow, The HIAB wasn't working properly, I had to unload everything myself, etc, etc.

Remember, there was very little to occupy us out there, so what seems the simplest of things in the UK was taken very seriously by us. One such thing was being sent on an errand, taking total advantage and taking three times as long as necessary to do it; then the icing on the cake – being thanked profusely for being so helpful. That really tickled me.

One particular morning, driving through Port Stanley coincided with the local children's time for walking to school. I didn't give it a second thought at the time. I suppose it was 'rush' hour. It was quite reassuring when I considered that this was a war zone less than two years ago, and there was still a lot of tidying up and rebuilding of lives and property to do, so the normality of children playing in the streets as they walked to school was a welcome sight. So I took great care and slowly made my way through the town. The schoolchildren didn't appear to be as streetwise as their counterparts in the UK, as they just weren't used to the volumes of traffic on a normal day. Equally, there were no pedestrian crossings or lollipop ladies, and pretty poor (if any) road markings, so it was wise to give the children a wide berth in case they saw a distraction and just ran across your path. Of course, this would be one of the many regrettable days that I didn't have my camera with me, but driving along St Mary's Walk, leading to John Street, I saw a bunch of about eight children ahead of me, probably about eight to ten years old, standing in a circle in the middle of the road, taking great interest in whoever or whatever they were surrounding. There always seemed to be one of them looking over their shoulder as they formed a close huddle, so it was safe to assume they were up to some prank. I stopped the lorry in the street and just waited until an adult pointed to the vehicle and gestured to the children that they should move away from the traffic. My own daughter was ten years old at the time, so I got to thinking about what would have made her and her friends back home get so excited and secretive about on their way to school on a freezing cold morning. Back home in Elgin, it most certainly wouldn't have been what I was just about to see.

All was revealed, unexpectedly, when the circle broke up and a confused little penguin emerged from the middle and started to waddle off down the street. He, or she, was a good 60 or 70 yards from the sea and, by the way the children skipped and followed it, I can't see how they'd have got to school in time. This was a very timely reminder that I was in the middle of a very different country and culture, and made me appreciate how lucky I was to witness it. I'm not sure the poor, wee penguin felt so lucky, as the children kept cutting off its path to the shore. I'm also convinced it would have thought twice about straying into town again.

Another thing I always made a point of stopping to look at when we walked into Port Stanley, and I can't believe I never ever took a photo, was on the seashore outside the abattoir on the opposite end of Port Stanley from the airfield. On certain days there was obviously a mass slaughtering and processing of cattle, which to our minds, from seeing movies, would be classed as steers. You know the type, with three-foot-long horns that stick straight out each side of their big, chunky heads, like motorbike handlebars. There would be about 10 or 12 complete heads with horns, just thrown into the sea. Certainly not a sight that your average vegetarian might appreciate, but pretty damn impressive when you come from a country where you rarely see a beast with horns at all.

So, the working day consisted of about a half mile lift in the back of a Bedford lorry in the morning, from the Coastel to the camp. The largest part of my day, unless out on a jaunt to weld on a Phantom aircraft out on the airfield, as mentioned earlier in this chapter, was spent in the workshop. There was just myself and a Sergeant, who was also a welder, so I was virtually left to my own devices while he did 'important' paperwork. The working day was 12 hours, 6 days a week. My day off was every Friday, my boss's was a Monday.

Now, life is only interesting when you can get up to some sort of scheming. I'll mention in a while my money-making scheme, which is always an incentive to work as far as I'm concerned. But to give me time to do it, I had a master plan. The RAF had a job card system to record jobs, materials and time, called the Form 4426. So if somebody wanted something legitimate making for their workplace, they raised a form which described the job, and we could record on it what materials we used from our stock, and how many manhours were spent on it. The job could then be costed to the department who requested the job.

Some days, people would come and ask for a piece of metal so that they could do their own job for their place of work, but it had to be recorded that the metal had gone to that department. No problem when they were genuine people needing metal for a genuine repair that they could do themselves. This is where the intelligent bit comes in. If someone wanted a bit of metal, I used to get them to sign a blank Form 4426 and I'd say I'd fill it in for them. No problem since everyone hates filling forms in. I then hid the undated form.

When my boss had his day off, I used to do all my cash-paying jobs, and then, as though by magic, all the blank, signed 4426s reappeared. I'd fill them in, write off the metal that was genuinely used, then fill in the manhours on several of them, which coincidentally added up to exactly twelve hours, and neatly stacked the forms in my boss's in-tray.

Next morning, he'd want an update on what had happened in his absence, and he always used to comment 'You had a busy old day yesterday, Graham, thanks very much for your support.' I always managed to keep a straight face and just told him that it was what I was here to do.

On one occasion, I pushed it to the limit. Not only did I do my own personal jobs and fictitiously claimed the twelve hours for that day, but I also chanced my luck and put down for fourteen hours. Sure enough, next morning he once again complimented me on my efforts, and I was told to make sure I took an extra two hours off to make up for it. Bosses like that are just a gift that keeps on giving.

I mentioned in Chapter One that Sir Rex Hunt, Governor of the Falkland Islands, had a red London taxi as his official car. It was quite a comforting and homely sight around the town, although not used excessively. However, one thing that maybe his staff shouldn't have been so trusting with, was bringing the taxi to us for a minor repair and a respray. Officially it was probably seen as an honourable gesture and token of our goodwill and respect, for the RAF to be able to help him out. I wonder what was going through his mind as to where his beloved car was, because it was like a magnet for us while it was in our care. I really hope nobody checked the mileage before it came in, because it seemed to do an awful lot of test driving around the base, and if there had been CCTV around at that time, oh dear, the amount of different

*Sir Rex Hunt's official car (complete with extra signage)*

drivers would have been clocked. As you can see in the photos, we felt obliged to put some signs on the car as a joke.

I can't quite remember where, but somewhere on the base hired out video cameras, probably the NAAFI shop. So we got hold of one and took this opportunity to hone our filming skills. Firstly, using the taxi, we made a Benny Hill type sketch where the car pulled up at the workshop and what appeared to be about 25 people got out of the back. Of course the other side of the car wasn't visible on the film, so the same six people went round and round and in the other open rear door.

The second film was about London cab drivers, so one 'passenger' sat in the back with the cameraman beside him. The competition was for best authentic sounding Cockney cab driver, so we were pretending to drive whilst having a conversation, coming out with all sorts of rhyming slang and references to Pearly Kings and Queens in true Chas and Dave style. I'm afraid that was one competition I couldn't win, as my Scottish accent doesn't transfer well to cockney, so I stuck to being the cameraman.

Yes, we did actually do some work and Sir Rex's car was duly returned to him repaired, resprayed, washed and valeted. The taxi served as official car for 34 years and was finally retired to Port Stanley museum in 2010.

I suppose the message I'm trying to portray is the working conditions and the whole set up of the camp were a transition between a war zone and a fully functioning Air Force base. One minute you're indoors, albeit in a tent, concentrating on welding a delicate aircraft part, then you step outside to go to your portakabin for a cup of tea, the rain is horizontal, it's cold every day and the footpath is a row of pallets because the field is so muddy.

I remember one day a consignment of acetylene cylinders was delivered to us. Normally, in the UK, nobody bothers with the forged-steel screw-on caps, but these were all capped. I thought I had nothing more to do than screw the cap off by hand and use the cylinder. This cap wouldn't move, not by hand, not with a chain wrench, not by hammering it. Eventually we had to heat it (not exactly recommended as it contains extremely flammable gas) and slowly we got it to turn. It transpires that, whoever was responsible for delivering it to the island, decided that it should go by sea on the open deck of a cargo ship, probably taking weeks to get there. So this thing was rusted solid after exposure to the sea air and then stored for goodness knows how long.

Before the days of mobile phones and laptops, the important job of finding out the football scores from the UK on a Saturday was done via the radio. Normally, back home, these started about 4.40 pm on a Saturday afternoon. With the five-hour time difference, we got them at 11.40 in the morning. Shouldn't be much of a problem, but lunch was at 12 noon, and I had to get washed, take off my boiler suit, walk about 200 yards and beat the queues. Quite a challenge, especially as the Scottish League results were always last, but the lure of food (breakfast had been at 6 am) ensured I got there on time. Saturday afternoons seemed weird though, it just didn't seem right doing an afternoon's work after hearing the scores.

Really, only three things differentiated any one day from another because the workload and working times were always the same, and we didn't have television. Friday was my day off so that was always looked forward to, although we had to get up just as early as a workday to make the most of the limited daylight hours. Saturday had the football results, so plenty of rivalry and banter at lunch time as the scores came in. And on Sundays there was no Hercules Airbridge from Ascension with the mail. Monday, I suppose could also count as a day for me to look forward to because my boss was off so that was my 'Do What You Want' day.

Another highlight of the day was the mail delivery. Blueys are blue paper tri-fold letters that are posted by airmail to and from the UK for free. Most people received and sent one every day, so it became a nice habit and ritual each afternoon, and it was comforting to think families back home were taking the trouble to do the same. Conversely, it hit you hard when you didn't get one as it was customary to gloat at someone with no mail, especially if you got two. There was only one plane, six days a week, Monday to Saturday, from Ascension Island, so if word got round that the plane either didn't leave Ascension, or turned back, usually due to bad weather, heads did go down a bit.

There was a great deal of one-upmanship with blueys as (and I haven't a clue who started this) everyone used to make shapes from cubes of rubber and use them as ink stamps to adorn the letter. Mostly animal figures were made, with penguins being the most popular. It was quite comical when people left the island to go home after their tour, as the first thing they'd be asked was whether they'd hand over their blueys ink stamp. If anyone had a date stamp in their desk, or just any random stamp laying around, someone would use it on a bluey, then it was customary to show it off to anyone and everyone.

My biggest claim to fame was visiting the Port Stanley Police Station one day, not in any capacity as a criminal (on this occasion), but to pick up some documents for the RAF Station. The policeman on duty wasn't very sure of what I had been sent to pick up, so he went round to a back room to telephone someone and left me at the front desk. Next thing I see is him walking to another building, so I felt really trusted and had a good look at my surroundings (first time in a Police station ever) and I felt like a kid in a sweet shop. I spotted a 'Falkland Islands Police Force' stamp, so I quickly pressed it on the ink pad and stamped a few blank blueys I had in my pocket. Imagine if I'd had the guts to steal it, what a result that would have been. Oh my word, madness must have been setting in, being away from home, on a remote South Atlantic freezing cold island, because my blueys were the talk of the camp, and other servicemen were soon trying to conjure up excuses to visit the Police Station. I suppose your average serviceman's visit to a Police Station bypasses the front desk and goes straight to the cells, so genuine visits would be few and far between. Several years later, in 1992, the Falkland Islands Police Force was granted the prefix 'Royal' by Queen Elizabeth II. Imagine the prestige of getting hold of that stamp.

Nowadays my compatriots at RAF Mount Pleasant won't have these sort of exciting pastimes as they WhatsApp their families back home.

Tea breaks and dinner breaks were always a time for a laugh and a get together in our canteen, situated between the Workshop and Ground Equipment Rubbs. Made up of portakabins, it was shared by about 20 of us on any given day. Obviously loads of stories were exchanged, often about the camp and the area, but also, get a heap of RAF guys together and they'll tell you their life stories. Sometimes it was good to be one of the quieter ones, like myself, and just sit back and take in some of the tales. And that includes the ones that definitely had to be taken with a pinch of salt.

Card games, whist and rummy, and darts were popular, and a couple of guys for a while started trying to get a table of bridge going. There were two servicemen who were decent at it and attempted to get about four others interested. I tried my best, and sort of held my own being one of the four novices, but the two good players took it a bit too seriously. One thing I used to enjoy was a little bit of winding them up, so it paid to play reasonably seriously for ten to fifteen minutes, then do something amazingly daft. This gave the serious guys time to think they were in a semi decent game, then there was nothing better than a good wind up. So, bridge starts with bidding with your partner to establish how many hands you think you'll win. From memory, I think you bid for how many hands over six you'll win, so if you bid seven, that means you'll hope to win six plus the seven, so all thirteen hands of cards. This was relatively rare, so a bridge expert would get excited about the possibility, although it would still take a bit of strategy between the pair to succeed. It wasn't a foregone conclusion. So the best test of character, is to play with a serious partner, bid to win all thirteen hands, get him excited about the tremendous hands of cards you must be sharing between you, then Wham!, lay down a card that you know will lose you the first hand. It won't be the first time I've seen the cards fly across the room, and it usually resulted in someone storming out of the canteen. Great fun, if you think some folk take life just a tad too seriously. Having one guy calling you all the names under the sun is worth it when the entire workforce are jeering and laughing their heads off.

Our workshop wasn't far from the shore, and there was a nice, sandy beach along a track that was fenced off from the potential minefields. Often at a lunchtime, some of us would go for a wander if we wanted a bit of fresh air, peace and quiet. We weren't allowed on the beach because that hadn't been certified as mine-free, but there was a viewing point at the end of the path where we could safely watch the penguins. Fortunately for them, the Magellanic and Gentoo penguins were deemed to be not heavy enough to trigger landmines, so although the beaches were sealed off to us from the landward side, the penguins could wander ashore relatively safely. Of course, there was always a serviceman somewhere who would try and impress with his tales of seeing penguins blown to smithereens in front of his eyes, but that was one of many stories to take with a copious amount of salt. The mine clearances (30,000 mines were laid by Argentinian Forces) were slow and ongoing at that time, and final clearance wasn't declared until November 2020. It was quite disconcerting, walking in certain areas where, several years previously, it would have been a pleasure to be taking in the views and enjoying a stroll on the beach, and now, post-war, seeing heavily fenced off footpaths and beach areas, with clear signage: DANGER – MINES. The wording of the warning signs in areas thought to be relatively safe still reinforced what a difficult task it would be to declare any area as mine-free, given that many beaches were affected by the tides:

'WARNING – Although this area is believed to be clear of mines, it is possible that a mine may be washed ashore from a nearby minefield. Please be careful. Do not touch any suspicious object, but place a marker nearby and report it.'

But back to the penguins, by far the most spectacular sight was watching the big waves, about 75 yards in front of me, breaking on the shore. As the wave reached its full height, the penguins swam across the front of the waves and could be easily seen darting through the crystal-clear water, just like looking through the glass on the side of an aquarium. Rarely did the penguins wander too far from the water's edge. I don't think we posed a particular threat to them, maybe it was because they were put off by the constant noise, vehicles and activity from the airfield.

Another memorable thing that happened one day on a lunchtime stroll was when I encountered an elusive long-tailed meadowlark (by the way I'm hardly what you'd call an enthusiastic ornithologist). My Dad always encouraged me to take an interest in wildlife, especially birds, and was forever pointing out birds, nests and eggs during childhood walks. Known locally as Robin Red Breast, but alternatively known to us as the Military Starling with the male's bright red breast, the long-tailed meadowlark was rarely spotted at close quarters, and they were ridiculously hard to photograph. If you think about a black-coloured bird, the size of our starling or male blackbird, but with a full-length red front, that's pretty close to the long-tailed meadowlark. When I'd first been told about them, I envisaged something like our robin, but these were way more majestic. So, imagine my astonishment when I'm ambling along on my way towards the beach, minding my own business, a million things going through my mind, and a chirping bird lands on a fencepost immediately on my left-hand side. This, of course, would be a day I was walking alone and no-one was with me to witness my claim. It stood so proudly, almost defiantly, chirping beside my ear, and I identified it straight away as I'd heard so much about the military starling. But instead of being a switched-on, keen amateur photographer with camera to hand, I had to reach into the inside pocket of my jacket and, as quickly as he arrived, he flew off at speed with the first movement of my arm. Needless to say I couldn't wait to tell everyone when I got back to work, but nobody believed me (nor seemed to care) when I told them what I had just seen. You believe me, don't you?

Finding things to do outwith work was crucial, as the days were long, so occupying yourself helped pass the time. Of course there were always characters who could sleep for Britain, and spending a day off sleeping was their idea of well-spent time off, but that seemed to me to be more than a bit of a waste of time. Being a country boy, I found it astonishing that there were many guys who took absolutely no interest in the geography, the views, or the wildlife surrounding them. This was a one-off opportunity to experience a land that we'd heard so much about and, potentially, anyone who returned for a second posting in years to come would probably end up in Mount Pleasant, the new purpose-built airfield and RAF camp being constructed 33 miles south-west of Port Stanley and due to be opened in 1985. So the ruggedness and basicness of the camp and the island was worth experiencing now; a one-off posting

The Falklands Ashtray    71

*Penguins from viewing point at the end of the runway.*

*Long tailed Meadow Lark (Military Starling)*
*Credit- pencil drawing by Julie Hemsley.*

and a great memory. Having been brought up in the Inner Hebrides made me just that bit more interested in island life.

First thing on your first day off was usually a walk into Port Stanley.

By the way, I'm sure locals would debate whether the town (town at that time but now a city) should be referred to by the official title of Stanley, or the popularised name of Port Stanley. We always referred to it as Port Stanley so that's what I've used throughout this book. Equally confusing were people who wrongly referred to the RAF camp as RAF Port Stanley, but actually RAF Stanley is, or was, the correct terminology. I suppose it was just over a mile, a very nice walk I have to say, but there was always a bitingly cold wind in what was now the height of winter. Unfortunately there were no trees, no dry-stone walls and no buildings to provide shelter from the wind or rain. Having been posted there, I obviously had no say whatsoever in the timing of my arrival, but I suppose if anyone chose to visit the Falklands, and had a free choice of dates, the month of May probably wasn't the cleverest month to start a visit. Just finishing spending a winter in the UK, followed by a winter in the Falklands, then home in October for winter in the UK again, wasn't ideal for my vitamin D exposure. I don't take a good suntan anyway, but by the Spring of 1985 I was as white as a sheet after three consecutive winters. Hitching a lift was an acceptable method of indicating that you'd appreciate being picked up, and even Service drivers, who normally would be instructed never to pick up a hitchhiker, were encouraged to do so. There was an unwritten understanding that any vehicle on the road would pick up anyone walking and most often, they did offer. If we were walking as a largish group we'd usually decline, unless we could all get in a lorry, but it was very welcome if walking alone in the cold. Port Stanley was more something to be experienced once or twice, rather than an exciting day out. Everyone had to go into the Falklands Store, where souvenirs were in abundance; plenty of tea towels, mugs, maps etc, etc all with the Falklands motifs and crests on them.

There was The Globe bar in Port Stanley and we were advised, but

The Falklands Ashtray 73

*West Store (Falkland Islands Company)*

*The Globe Hotel*

not ordered, not to go there, not for any trouble it would cause, but I could totally understand a small town (actually a city as from 14th June 2022) with less than a couple of thousand residents not being happy with suddenly having their population greatly increased with a functioning Air Force base on their doorstep. Literally scores of servicemen wandering about every day would find it tempting to pop in for a pint, and the locals deserved their peace and quiet as we had our own bars on camp. Our prices were very favourable, maybe that was deliberate, and we wouldn't feel the need to go off camp for a drink (mind you, a cool pint versus lukewarm tins of beer was very tempting).

The 1982 Liberation Memorial was completed and unveiled by Sir Rex Hunt during my stay, so that was worth seeing and paying our respects at. Otherwise, Port Stanley was just a very colourful town, nice to walk around on a summer's afternoon I'm sure, but the chill winds made it very uncomfortable, so sightseeing was hurried rather than relaxed. There were a few iconic things and places to take obligatory photos of, namely Whalebone Arch (jawbones of two blue whales brought to the Falklands from the South Shetland Islands in Antarctica, to commemorate 100 years of British administration in 1933), Christ Church Cathedral, the red phonebox complete with old fashioned phone with A and B buttons, Government House and Sir Rex Hunt's infamous red London taxi.

We were never certain how we'd be received by locals. There certainly wasn't any of the hysteria and flag-waving that Prime Minister Maggie Thatcher got, and the feeling was that we were tolerated rather than welcomed with open arms. Fully understandable really, we were like a mini (peaceful) invasion every day, and people were just wanting to get back to normal, as they were still rebuilding their lives in their quiet, isolated community.

*St. Mary's Catholic Church*

*Christ Church Cathedral & Whalebone Arch*

Of course, we had to have nicknames for each other. In the Services it's almost compulsory. These were still the days where nobody challenged sensitive nicknames, many that you simply wouldn't get away with now. But Dusty (Miller), Lofty (Short Guy), Taffy (Welshman), Jock (Scotsman) were typically innocent and said without malice. Our

Warrant Officer at GEF in Wattisham, W/O Grant, was funny. You could tell his mood swings by your chosen name that day:

'McTavish!' he'd shout to me. That meant he was in a jovial mood.

'Jock!' was an average way of beckoning me for something work related.

'Logie!' Oh Oh, I jumped to his every command, that meant he wasn't pleased at all.

Being a damn cold place, it seemed every local in the Falklands wore a woolly hat. Crossroads (renamed Crossroads Motel in 1985) was still a very popular early evening soap-opera on television back home, and one of the most loveable characters was Benny Hawkins (not the sharpest tool in the toolbox), played by Paul Henry, who was never without his woolly hat. So islanders, who historically had been called 'Kelpers', after the seaweed they traditionally harvested, affectionately became known as 'Bennies'. This didn't go down too well, as the Service's hierarchy deemed it insulting rather than affectionate, and I suppose today it would have been an example of political incorrectness, so servicemen were instructed that the nickname was controversial and disrespectful and we should refrain from using it. Unfortunately, servicemen are like children. When told not to do something, you either keep doing it, or find a way round it. And so islanders became known as 'Stills' because they were 'still Bennies'. The authorities were on a hiding to nothing though, because if we received any further bans, we had plenty of other spare nicknames to use, 'SAB' (still a Benny), 'TSB' (they're still Bennies), and, probably the cleverest one, 'Andies' (and 'es still a Benny).

Not to be outdone, we found out that the islanders had a nickname for RAF guys. Historically, and I can't deny, it's absolutely accurate, when airmen get talking amongst themselves there's a protocol where the more you've experienced in your career, and that usually means the more camps you've been stationed at, the more superior you feel and the more likely you are to impress by making fun of less experienced guys. So conversations and statements may typically and monotonously start with, 'When I was in Cyprus …' or, 'When I was on detachment in Nevada …' or, 'When I was with the Red Arrows …' and now of course, 'When I was in the Falklands …'.

Very quickly, the islanders decided, if locals were going to be known as 'Bennies', then RAF guys who appeared to start every conversation with 'When I' were going to be called 'When I's' or, in rhyming parlance, 'Whennies'.

I was very fortunate to have the same day off as three guys from our work area who were much more experienced hill walkers than I was, but not to the extent that they were like mountain goats and would leave me trailing behind. Rather, they enjoyed the outdoors, were a damn sight fitter than me, and were fairly experienced map readers. I honestly don't think I'd have had the time or motivation to organise full days out if I'd been left to my own devices or if my days off had coincided with different colleagues. Something I'm convinced I've got in common with ex-servicemen throughout the country is remembering their damn names 40 years later. I can remember Ken Pick and Ian Cook, but the third name escapes me and that really frustrates me. The three of them, especially Cookie, were also very confident and forthright and weren't afraid to ask anyone for anything, so they quickly found out what was on offer, who were the right people to ask, and what help we could get from the RAF. We got our heads together one evening not long after getting to the Falklands, and since they were pretty damn good at organising things, we soon had a plan to trek every few weeks to different hills and locations that we were acquainted with through hearing them being mentioned in news bulletins during the war.

78    The Falklands Ashtray

*Liberation Memorial*

*Ken, Cookie and I (seated) on Windy Ridge*

The Mess kitchens happily provided us with pack lunches, and an RAF Land Rover would drive us through Port Stanley and beyond a couple of miles around the Moody Brook estuary area, to the start of our walks, provided we were an organised group, carried a radio and left details of where we were going and our expected return times. I think the Services in general were very sympathetic and supportive to anyone who constructively used their free time. It was better than having dozens of guys floating aimlessly around the streets all day in pursuit of a pint.

In the mountains around Port Stanley, there were many vantage points where Argentinian and British Forces had made camp and, judging by what they left behind, some were vacated pretty rapidly. If you were lucky, there were still some that were totally untouched and, as you can see by some of my photos, the odd ones had several, uncollectable items, but more often than not, trophy hunters had stripped them bare of anything vaguely militaria. It was still interesting to see how they'd camouflaged themselves into the hillsides, and the odd articles of clothing and equipment that were still laying around. It was also interesting to sit with maps and get our bearings, relative to Port Stanley, to try and work out how the position fitted into the attacks and ultimate re-taking of the town.

None of these positions were recorded or plotted on any maps, so it was a case of potluck if you came across one. It was standard practice for us to report any findings to the RAF about the location of such shelters. Sometimes we could have a good, educated guess at where the best place would be to set up an attacking encampment, and if you guessed right, it was pretty satisfying. There were tales of colleagues, who were first on the scene immediately after the war, finding weapons and ammunition, but as these servicemen had gone home a long time ago, stories and claims were difficult to prove. I'm sure some stories had an element of truth, especially those who claimed to have found and kept weapons in the very early days, but after a couple of pints in the bar, some extra 'finds' were invented. 'Pull up a sandbag' stories were rife as servicemen loved outdoing each other.

80   The Falklands Ashtray

*Mt Tumbledown pickings*

*Gun on Wireless Ridge*

So, a typical day (and we were extremely fortunate that virtually every hillwalking day was cold, but dry and sunny) would be to collect our lunches, radios and maps at first light, and get the Land Rover to drop us off about one or two miles west of Port Stanley. There was Sapper Hill and Mount Tumbledown to the south of the road, and Wireless Ridge, Mount Longdon and Two Sisters Ridge to the north.

We were briefed on a few things. Firstly, the Air Force was pretty good at helping us plan our walks, and telling us of areas to avoid because of uncharted or potential minefields. Secondly, we were given the current forecast and always warned of incredible potential changes in weather conditions. The weather, unfortunately, and embarrassingly, turned out to be our downfall one day. We were returning from Mount Longdon and attempting to reach a track which would take us along the shore at Wireless Ridge and then onwards to Port Stanley for our planned pick-up point at a small bridge over Moody Brook. We'd been a bit overenthusiastic in trying to see as much of Mount Longdon as possible, and underestimated the time it would take us to descend. Sure enough, the wind and rain just blew up from nowhere, and an enjoyable brisk walk suddenly turned into a battle to even see where we were going. Time just disappeared, darkness was falling, but at least we were in radio contact with the camp and our transport.

A perfect day out on a sun-drenched hillside really turned quite frightening as we realised we couldn't possibly safely reach our intended rendezvous point. But as luck would have it, it was quickly established that there was an RAF Sea King helicopter doing some work at the foot of Wireless Ridge and it was going to return to the airfield in case it became weather-bound. We could hear the helicopter rotors so headed towards it and, in now almost complete darkness, it's array of lights were a most welcome sight. We boarded it and were promptly ferried the two miles,

82   The Falklands Ashtray

*Argentinian stretcher alongside bomb crater*

*88mm gun in front of Two Sisters*

in probably just over three minutes, across the harbour to the airfield. So I suppose we were officially rescued, as we couldn't see how we'd have walked back to where we should have been in such atrocious conditions. The helicopter crew said they wouldn't be going anywhere else after landing, which emphasises just how wild it became. However, it was a great exercise in hill walkers following all the rules and the authorities offering great advice and help. I'm sure it was a very mundane hop across the bay for the crew, but a textbook rescue in our eyes. I think we just got too greedy while up on Mount Longdon and, even after finding a couple of spots where the military had dug into the hillside, it became infectious that you just kept wanting to find one more outpost, hoping you'd find something that no-one else had discovered. It certainly ensured we made better plans and stuck to them in future walks.

It also made us realise just how difficult things must have become during the war, which was during the same months, two years previously. We were used to seeing pictures of soldiers high up on the hills on sunny, cold days. Everyone was becoming aware of the term 'yomping', and there are some iconic photos of soldiers carrying the flag towards Port Stanley, but we hadn't appreciated that on top of their achievements a lot would have been carried out under atrocious and changeable weather conditions.

Sapper Hill was probably the least eventful but easiest walk, although there were some lovely views over Port Stanley and the harbour, as well as some of the coastline beyond the harbour entrance.

Two Sisters Ridge and Mount Tumbledown were by far the most enjoyable walks, as the scenery was amazing and both areas were very well known to us in as much as we'd heard such a lot about them during the war. The Battle of Mount Tumbledown was legendary, and one of the last positions to be taken before eventual reclaiming of the Falklands from the Argentinians.

A couple of days before the Battle of Mount Tumbledown, the Battle of Two Sisters was equally infamous as a three-pronged attack, along with Mount Harriet and Mount Longdon, which aided the British Army's advance on Port Stanley.

A noise I hear from time to time over the years, and which immediately reminds me of days hillwalking in the Falklands, is the noise of a Chinook helicopter. Nicknamed the Wokka, the sound of its two rotors is unmistakable, and there was no nicer introduction to a day's walking in the cold and the sun, than hearing a Chinook miles away in the distance and heading towards us at low level from the Mount Kent direction, along Moody Brook (between the mountains mentioned above). The 'Wokka Wokka' sound getting closer and louder is unique and was quite inspirational, especially in that circumstance, as the noise echoed from the hills on either side.

# Chapter Four
## – Coffins

Unfortunately, the next experience was one I never expected, and I hope I can touch on it sensitively, but it turned out to be something I'll never forget and something I now feel honoured that I could do for others.

Enough of the mystery, the strange title of the chapter gives it away. The task I had to complete was sealing zinc coffins once bodies being flown home to the UK had been placed in them. It was certainly a job that put everything around you into perspective. Someone's sad, final trip home.

Nothing could ever have set me up for this. My posting to the Falklands was quite rushed, and I left Scotland a few weeks earlier than expected. This was because the guy I was replacing had to leave early and so he and I had no handover. We probably passed each other in the South Atlantic somewhere and, unless he was fortunate enough to have got a flight in the daily Hercules, he was probably being bounced around on the MV *Keren*, so bad luck with that one, my friend.

As a result, he couldn't pre-warn me that one of the many and varied jobs I'd have to undertake would be soldering zinc coffin lids. So many of us have this weird concept of working with human remains. Tell a welder to solder a box and he'll do it. Second nature. Tell him there's a body in the box and it becomes much more nerve wracking.

When a body is flown home it has to be in a sealed metal container. Basically, the body is placed in a body bag, then laid in a zinc coffin, which in turn is placed in a mock coffin, i.e. a plywood replica coffin which respectfully looks like the genuine article, but is only for show during transportation. The decorative handles are not weight-bearing. The mock coffin is then put in a wooden crate, with four-inch-thick horsehair padding around it, for loading onto the aircraft.

This was the normal procedure, which we didn't question. In fact we didn't really know at the time who instigated it or why it needed to be done this way. I've since learned that there have been various international agreements for repatriation of bodies by air, and we were following the second such agreement entitled The Agreement on the Transfer of Corpses (Strasbourg – 1973). Article 6 requires that the coffin must travel in the hold of an aircraft, and be provided with a device to balance the internal and external pressures, namely an internal, soldered zinc coffin, and that the coffin should be packaged in a way that it no longer resembles a coffin, i.e. a wooden crate.

Bodies were kept in cold storage in the morgue, affectionately referred to as 'the Fridge', and operated by Army personnel.

When the aircraft was due to land, the route and the service was called the Airbridge by the way, the finely polished process of preparation began.

An RAF Hercules C-130 aircraft would leave Ascension Island for the daily journey south. After it took off there were three opportunities for it to abort the journey if it encountered any issues. One was that it could turn back under its own steam, provided it had used less than half its fuel. Another opportunity was that, if it had gone further, a Victor or Hercules tanker aircraft could meet it and offer refuelling to enable it to return. The third chance was, and this was the least favoured, that it could divert to Rio de Janeiro in Brazil if the weather closed in rapidly at RAF Stanley. After flying further south than Rio, there came a 'point of no return'.

Once it had committed to that point, it simply had to land at RAF

Stanley, so accurate advanced weather forecasting was critical. If the Hercules was definitely coming, and, equally important, that the forecast looked like it would be able to take off again successfully, the coffin transportation procedure could commence. Otherwise the body had to remain in cold storage.

We'd get notification in an evening that, the next morning, a body was to be flown home. The aircraft would pass the point of no return and we'd get confirmation. Landing time was usually about 11 am. By the time the Hercules landed, refuelled, disembarked and took on passengers, fed the crew, and offloaded and reloaded cargo, she would potentially take off again about 2 pm. So everything we did was timed so that we finished soldering the coffin (which was already inside the mock coffin), the plywood lid was attached, and the coffin then placed in the large, wooden, purpose-built, palleted crate, just in time for it to be the last item loaded onto the plane.

The procedure was that the Army medics would remove the body, which was in a body bag, from the Fridge, into the zinc coffin, within the plywood coffin. An unmarked vehicle would then transport the coffin to our now lovely, tidy workshop, where we placed two trestles in the middle of the floor ready to receive the coffin. Apart from tidying the workshop, we had some blue curtains that we hung around the workshop floor space to hide as much machinery as possible, but there was little else we could do to make the place any less industrial and more respectful. Once in place in the workshop, we made sure everything and everybody showed respect, so no noisy work going on in the surrounding area, minimal vehicles were permitted to drive past the door, all radios turned off, a few people were positioned around the workshop to ensure no-one came barging in, and then a portable wooden screen was placed around us.

On rare occasions, family members would fly out to escort the body home. That was a tough shift, with grieving relatives rightly observing every move. Sometimes they'd bring a couple of floral tributes, but it gave us a sense of doing something worthwhile and it was appreciated when they always took the trouble to thank us. The padre, a military policeman, and a couple of Army or RAF officers not necessarily connected to the deceased, would accompany the entourage, just to give a more formal and dignified send off.

It was probably my one big complaint and grievance about our superiors, that no-one prewarned us about undertaking such a job, and we certainly hadn't been trained for it. Nowadays there's, correctly, a fuss made about working conditions, mental health and training, and yet young mechanical engineers were expected to just slot into such a delicate task. Far from not wanting to do it, I was humbled at being able to play my part in the safe, respectful repatriation of someone's loved one.

So with the screen in place, and yet another final re-confirmation from Operations that the flight would definitely be leaving today, the task could commence. This wasn't a job for little electrical soldering irons. We used traditional oxy-acetylene burners, like flame throwers, to heat heavy copper soldering irons to soft solder round the entire top edge of the zinc coffin. It would take me about 30 or 40 minutes to complete. The process was always explained fully beforehand to anyone accompanying the coffin, especially family, because we had to be in boilersuits and it sounded quite industrial with the burners and light hammering, considering this was such a sombre time.

Then, when we finished and confirmed the metal to be stone cold, the plywood lid was secured on top and the coffin placed inside the wooden crate, which was made secure by the carpenters.

By now, as you can imagine with the zinc coffin included, it was extremely heavy, and unfortunately, although maybe not the most elegant or respectful way to transport it to the plane, a four-wheel-drive, all-terrain forklift truck was used. This way, it was taken directly to the aircraft door and loaded aboard the Hercules, now ready for take-off. Our final small token of respect, that everyone involved participated in, was to stand at the roadside, in a sort of mini guard of honour, as the forklift drove away.

One thing that happened on one occasion, and again it emphasises that, at the time, people weren't so hot on welfare issues, a young forklift driver appeared at the workshop door, bang on time to take a coffin to the waiting aircraft. As far as he was concerned, his instructions were to pick up a crate at Station Workshops and take it to the plane. He rolled up to the workshop door, and, since no-one prewarned him, he was whistling to his heart's content before shouting some banter such as, 'Get a move on then.'

His mood quickly changed when he saw medics, the Padre, engineers, officers and a couple of tearful relatives, all in the doorway. The whole procedure was carried out respectfully, but there was always a sombre atmosphere about the place, which the driver obviously picked up on. As he slid the forklift into the pallet, he asked what was in the crate. Someone whispered to him that it was a body, and I felt so sorry for the youngster. He went white as a sheet, switched off the engine, jumped off the forklift and said, 'No way, no way, that's no way to handle a body,' and he just walked off. Needless to say a replacement driver was hurriedly made available, but what a state the poor guy got himself into.

Later on in the day, a few of us went to find the youngster. Obviously not the most worldly-wise young man. We emphasised to him that this was the only feasible way to lift such a heavy object and transport it about three or four hundred yards over a bumpy road. By now, totally calm, he just said that the whole ambiance about the workshop that day was a bit of a shock and not what he was expecting at all. In his opinion, it was no way to treat a body, but we explained to him that there wasn't really any better or alternative way to do it and we all, as a team, did everything we could to ensure the deceased was handled respectfully and safely. We convinced him that it was better disguised as a crate than looking like a coffin being forklifted up the road. Hopefully a vital lesson learned for his superiors.

On a slightly lighter note, I admit, money was tight in those days, so any opportunity to make money was always welcome, but also any time you felt aggrieved that someone else got money that you felt entitled to, it hurt a bit. So, slightly tongue in cheek, but with some frustration too, I always used to question why Army medics got £0.65 every time they handled a body, but we received nothing extra for what I deemed to be an extraordinary job. By calculation, 65p in 1984 is the equivalent of £2.58 in 2024. And I'm not talking about 65p for one repatriation. I'm talking about £0.65 to pick up a body from an accident scene. The same money to take it into the medical centre. Again 65p to take it from the medical centre to the morgue. The same to put it in the fridge, and again, the same to take it out, and the same to take it to the workshop. On a couple of occasions, the plane either broke down, or the weather prevented taking off, just before we started sealing the coffin, so the body went back. So £0.65 to take it back out of the workshop and the same to rechill it. And so it goes on. It may seem petty, but also it seemed weird for us not to be recognised for what we did. As far as our job descriptions went, I think it could be referred to as going the extra mile, and not your average run of the mill general engineering task. Also, today, with such a task, I shudder to think what would happen if something went wrong during the soldering. It's not inconceivable, for example, that the coffin could have been set on fire if anyone had been careless enough. In modern suing culture, people doing jobs without proper training is a godsend to a good lawyer. Totally unlikely, I know, but these were the grey areas in the three-year transition between war conditions in temporary facilities and a return to normal working at a purpose-built Air Force base.

This next couple of paragraphs may not be everyone's cup of tea, but it's no use telling a story as it was if you're not going to include the controversial bits. I have a very logical and pretty matter-of-fact view on death.

It's pretty damn certain that death is going to happen to an awful lot of us, and we, as a workshop group (engineers and carpenters) chose humour as our way of coping with a very delicate task. Nothing disrespectful, and anything that exists in someone's mind or behind closed doors is ok in my view.

An RAF carpenter and I were usually the ones most involved in sealing the coffins and making the wooden transportation crates. After each coffin left the workshop, and we did six during our tour, we used to record our 'achievement'. He had made a small, maybe a foot in length, wooden plaque in the shape of a coffin, and I made a coffin-shaped metal plate about an inch long, with a metal handle. I heated the metal plate till almost red hot, then 'branded' the wooden plaque each time. It used to hang behind the door on the workshop office wall, not in public view, but was our little piece of humour to lighten the day. Not being medics or undertakers, being in such close proximity to coffins was particularly mentally draining.

People often ask who the bodies were that were transported home, and although I think I was blissfully unaware of most of the names, I remember one was an unfortunate serviceman who was accidentally struck by a helicopter blade. Four, from memory, were also servicemen who died of natural causes. And the sixth one, a merchant seaman, was quite a unique story because we followed his journey from start to finish, so to speak. Without television, radio channels were our best way of keeping up with events, and one evening, there was an announcement on the international segment of the news on local radio that a container ship's load had shifted in heavy seas around Cape Horn, and unfortunately two crewmen lost their lives. The ship, as the broadcast went on to tell us, was steaming towards the Falkland Islands to facilitate the landing of one body for flying home to the UK. I don't know the country of registration of the ship, or the nationality of the crew, but, bizarrely, the family of the other crewmen elected to have him buried at sea. Firstly, I didn't think that was the done thing anymore, and, secondly, I can't imagine the process for confirmation of death etc. I can only imagine the body was landed ashore and medics and police confirmed burial could go ahead, before returning to sea, but again, something we heard about then never sought any details.

I heard the announcement of the container ship's accident while in my room and, on hearing that the body was to be landed in Port Stanley for repatriation to the UK, I went to tell my carpenter colleague about it. I met him in the corridor, coming the other way to inform me. The progress of the ship was tracked on radio each evening, as was the eventual helicoptering of the body to Port Stanley. It just seemed right to have the honour and opportunity to seal his coffin and bid farewell to him on his final journey after hearing so much about it.

Whilst on the subject of listening to the radio, the Falkland Islands Radio Service (FIRS) broadcast all the local news every evening. You could catch snippets of international stuff too, but local news and events were by far the most entertaining, especially the nightly roundup of movements next day on FIGAS, the Falkland Islands Government Air Service. A six-seater de Havilland Beaver aircraft and an eight-seater Britten-Norman Islander aircraft were used to ferry people around the islands in a glorified round robin taxi service. There were many landing strips on various islands, I believe about 30, and if you could endure the broadcast without falling asleep, the names, destinations and reasons for all travellers were announced across the airwaves.

So, for example, Mrs Smith, travelling from this island to that island, for medical appointment. Or, Mr P Brown, the vet, travelling from here to there, for pet surgery. These would be typical announcements and I'm sure very interesting if you were involved or if you knew the people concerned, but pretty mundane for those of us not participating. Also, I suppose, interesting if you were really nosey. Just think, if you wanted to avoid someone, you had prior warning that they were coming in on tomorrow's plane. Better still, if your boss had to travel by plane to your place of work, there was no way he was going to sneak up on you.

I've thought a lot about mental health, or mental ill-health to be more accurate. Troops have gone through all sorts of hardships in wars worldwide over the years and I'm not suggesting for a minute that we endured anything like that, but when I consider how far we've come as a nation in recent years, I think back to how relatively recent the Falklands conflict was, and yet we were a lot less clued up on mental well-being. Sealing the coffins, to me, is a prime example with no-one giving a thought as to whether we were prepared for such a thing, and no thought given to whether we wanted a break to gather our thoughts afterwards. Okay, we had packed lunches brought to us each time, but that was more because the plane times always coincided with when we should have gone to the Mess for lunch, rather than because anybody considered if we needed a breather and a bit of down time.

The poor youngster who leapt off the forklift became a bit of a laughingstock, and the story was relayed as a joke for many weeks after. Nowadays, someone like that would be offered counselling of some sort, and rightly so. And I would hope that any non-medical personnel would at least be informed as to the contents of a crate when it contained a body, and respectfully asked if they objected to handling it.

Before retirement, I was a trade union Shop Steward, and my current training and appreciation of mental ill-health means I would appreciate and challenge any instances I saw of people not being treated with respect and given aftercare, much more now than was the norm back in the 1980s. Another couple of instances I witnessed emphasise this.

In our workshop in RAF Lossiemouth, we had a section that we shared with electricians. One guy in particular was a very highly-strung individual and a definite loner. He was as skinny as a rake and shook like a leaf all day long. Everyone just treated him as weird but, looking back, he must have been inundated with issues going on inside him. Anyway, he was selected to go to the Falklands about a month before me, and the general feeling amongst colleagues was 'good riddance' rather than 'good luck'. One day, he was working on a piece of equipment and pieces of circuit board had to be glued to a metal panel. At that time we used Bostik glue all the time, and anyone who can remember how overpowering the fumes were from that will appreciate the workshop absolutely stank of the stuff. Much better ventilation would be required nowadays. Now, I've smelled the top of a glue tin to identify if it was Bostik and it brought more than a tear to my eyes, so you can imagine me passing our friend and seeing him cup his hands around a Bostik tin and taking a huge sniff. I couldn't believe my eyes, and fully expected him to keel over. Instead, he turned to me, stopped shaking and smiled, saying, 'That's better.'

I realised this was a guy with a very serious problem, although glue sniffing and general solvent abuse were relatively unknown to us at the time.

I'd heard enough about what we were to expect in the Falklands to know that this guy was going be a liability to the RAF, and to himself, if he went on his upcoming tour, so I did something I'd never done before, and was completely alien to me, and reported him to our Officer in charge.

I found out a couple of days later that he'd been withdrawn from going to the Falklands, but again, thinking about it now, there wasn't any apparent aftercare, he was just left to keep bumbling through his job daily, looking a proper wreck. The priority was obviously to stop him going to the Falklands and becoming a liability and a hazard, rather than how he could be helped with his obvious reliance on solvents.

Another incident I saw in the Falklands was a serviceman, much more senior in rank to me, crying his eyes out and missing home. One lunchtime I was walking round the back of our workshop, and in the distance, towards the shore, I could see a crouched, motionless figure. Nosiness made me walk over and I could hear the sobbing before I could see the tears. It transpires that he'd calculated on a map the exact direction of the UK from where he was sitting, and he felt closest to his children when he sat in that spot. I bring this up purely to emphasise the sadness in the story, because I had to promise not to tell anyone, and it's not so many years ago that counselling was pretty much frowned upon, and I know from being in the Services at that time, that a good many people in responsible positions would have told this senior NCO to man-up and get his act together, rather than sit and talk things through with him.

# Chapter Five
# – Entertainment

The evening's entertainment was brilliant if your ambition was just to stand at the bar in The Shed, in a portakabin, outside the Coastel door, with ambient temperature (warmish) cans (no draught) of beer.

Once a week, we ran our own bingo in the Coastel canteen, which often turned into chaos or hysterics. The purple rinse brigade who frequent bingo halls in the UK, would shudder to hear or understand the bingo ball numbers rhyming slang being used. About the only clean one I can recite was when number 23 was called. This squadron was the resident Phantom Squadron at RAF Stanley, and, because they were based in hangars near the runway, they were separated from the main camp buildings. That meant we hardly saw each other, so meeting up in the canteen at night was a source of great rivalry and friendly banter. As a result, when number 23 was called at bingo, instead of 'two and three, twenty-three' being the call, it became 'two and three, 23 Squadron' and this was followed by an array of grunts, high pitched squeals and monkey impersonations, showing just what we thought of them. As I say, friendly banter, which they claimed was because of their incredible popularity.

The bingo had no great structure or purpose, and the cash prizes were rubbish. Being the bingo caller wasn't an honour or ambition, more a case of leaving yourself wide open to a tirade of verbal abuse. And all this taking place in the alcohol-free Coastel, so disputes and hard luck stories of how someone was robbed of a full house were continued in The Shed bar outside the Coastel in the later evening.

One thing I do have the utmost respect and thanks for, was when celebrities of the day volunteered to come out to the Falklands to put on a free show. The biggest name by far was comedian Jim Davidson. Jim had us in hysterics throughout his show with his 'nick-nick' and 'Chalky' routines and really encouraged audience participation. He was the master of the put-down line if anyone was brave enough to heckle him. One of the biggest cheers of the concert was when he really got stuck into his Police routines and some electricians in the audience activated a blue, flashing, battery-operated light that they'd brought. Jim really appreciated that effort and it just got him rambling on with more tales.

I was thrilled when I managed to contact Jim, and even more so when he agreed to endorse this book with a comment on how much he enjoyed visiting the Falklands. I think we forget that as well as the obvious entertainment value for us, these shows gave the entertainers the chance to feel involved in what was a massive operation by the British Forces.

Singer Tricia Dusky also appeared. Unknown to us beforehand, but a great performance, and again, what guts it must have taken to voluntarily choose to travel eight thousand miles to play a venue like this.

Two other famous faces to grace our stage were Tommy Vance and Richard Digance. Richard showed his true friendly personality to me recently by replying to my request for a quote in endorsement of this book and wishing me well with the publishing. He wasn't known to many of us at the time, apart from a few Londoners. My boss, a sergeant in Station Workshops, hailed from Ilford and he was very aware of Richard's career. He'd started his career in a club in Ilford in the late 1960s and in the 1970s he was touring and supporting acts like Jethro Tull, Tom Jones (now of course, Sir Tom), Elkie Brooks, Supertramp and Joan Armatrading. He made his television breakthrough a year after visiting us, and I always made a point of watching him. He credits a lot of his television success to his great friend Jim Davidson, about whom he famously said when referring to entertaining the troops, 'Jim always wants to go where there's trouble, and if there isn't any, he'll start some.'

Richard was famed as a singer-songwriter, mostly humorous original numbers. I immediately latched on to his dry sense of humour. Forty years on, I still remember, word for word, his opening line on stage. He got an average welcoming applause, mainly because no-one had ever heard of him, stood by the microphone, guitar in hand, and just stared, poker-faced at us. Then he said, 'I'm actually a wine aficionado. I love the white.' And then he smirked and stood in silence for 20 seconds, which is quite brave in front of an all-male, half-drunk audience, starved of entertainment. Then he said, 'Oh, red, yes red, I like that too.'

We all thought 'Is this guy for real?' Then he burst into his repertoire of original songs and received a standing ovation at the end. He was brilliant, just the lift we needed.

We really appreciated the fact that the performers put on shows for the many small outposts, as well as the bigger stage in RAF Stanley, and as Richard jokingly recalls, 'I flew 8,000 miles and performed to 8 British soldiers at San Carlos. It was my first ever sell-out concert.'

Tommy Vance had some amazing stories of meeting world-famous rock bands. Would you believe his real name was Richard Anthony Crispian Francis Prew Hope-Weston, which he abbreviated to Rick West during his early working life. He inherited the random name Tommy Vance while working on KOL Seattle radio station in 1964. He was virtually an unknown then, and he replaced another DJ called Tommy Vance who let the station down unexpectedly. Since they'd invested so much money in jingles with the name Tommy Vance on them, he was asked if he minded using that name, and it stuck. He used the name to his advantage by cryptically using his initials and calling himself 'TV on the radio'. He was known to many as a pirate radio station DJ as well as being a familiar voice on the British Forces Broadcasting Service (BFBS), so he was made very welcome. Although not a touring performer, taking the time and trouble to come to the Falklands earned our respect.

Something I never envisaged at the time was what went into creating a show like this. The acts appeared onstage and carried out a professional performance, but this wasn't a purpose-built studio in London, this was Jim Davidson, a National Treasure and accompanying entourage, bringing 5 tons of equipment, and performing 8,000 miles from home in a basic theatre in Coastel 3. Believe me, there was nothing basic about the show they put on: great sound, great lighting equipment and thoroughly entertaining. There's a classic video on YouTube with Jim, accompanied by dancers, singing a song written by Roy Wood, 'California Man', at this concert.

Jim's DVD account of the trip reads as:

Follow Jim Davidson to a dot in the South Atlantic, that two years prior, was the scene of conflict.

MISSION: To transport Jim Davidson, five musicians, four dancers, singers, film crew, and five tons of equipment, 8,000 miles to the Falklands.

THURSDAY 20TH SEPTEMBER 1984: Ascension Island: a volcanic rock 5 miles by 9 miles (small), accommodation – a portacabin (very small) with 24 bunks (cramped) and us (battery hens).

SATURDAY 22ND SEPTEMBER 1984: Port Stanley, another portacabin. The concert is held in a Coastal (floating barracks). Our little concert party is tremendous …

WEDNESDAY 26TH SEPTEMBER 1984: Chopper to Byron Heights; the pilot nearly couldn't find the top in all the mist …

FRIDAY 28TH SEPTEMBER 1984: The inevitable helicopter to

Goose Green, the most emotive concert we do. Jim's energy after so many long concerts is almost bionic ...

SATURDAY 29th SEPTEMBER 1984: Back to Stanley – and home.

Ok, the RAF had to transport everything and everyone around the islands for them, but it was still a great effort by the visiting volunteer performers. It was said that Jim Davidson pleaded with Margaret Thatcher to be the first entertainer in the Falklands after the war, and for years afterwards he repeated his efforts in other war settings, such as Afghanistan and Iraq.

As we got more settled into life there, we arranged an evening's entertainment of our own in the canteen at work. This was the 1984 RAF Stanley General Engineering Flight (GEF) Inaugural Fancy Dress Party. Maybe this was the first, but probably not the only, fancy dress event in RAF Stanley. I'm sure someone will start a debate and will correct my ignorance.

This first attempt, which everyone rolled their eyes at and said would never work, turned out better than I'd anticipated. Party makes it sound really grand; it was just tins of beer (left outside to chill), plates of sausage rolls and a few of us dressed up. I was really struggling to think of anything to dress up in, given the limited resources, and some of the airmen that appeared that night really deserve credit for their invention, especially the guy who turned himself into a domino for the night. He caused one of the biggest laughs of the night because he came into the canteen with his domino box costume intact and only his head and legs sticking out. Someone teased him by holding a glass of beer in front of his face saying, 'Sorry, I would offer you a drink, but you've no arms.' The room erupted when he punched out two carefully concealed holes at shoulder height and his arms appeared. He grabbed the guy's glass and downed it in one.

Now I'm always one to take an easy way out, in fact I couldn't really be bothered because I probably hadn't worn any fancy dress costume since Halloween when I was about 12 years old, and I thought the occasion would be a flop. I couldn't imagine where people could rustle up costumes in a place like this, and we hadn't time to have clothing or costumes sent from home, but a great coincidence happened about two days before the party. I was at work and this guy walks in asking me for help to repair a washing machine part. We got talking and I found out he worked in the Coastel laundry. That shouldn't really have been difficult for me to work out, considering there's a clue in what he asked for – who else would bring a washing machine part!

The subject of the fancy dress party came up for some bizarre reason and we joked, or at least I did, about how on earth could anyone make costumes with the limited time and resources we had. Anyway, he said that he shouldn't really do this, and I looked trustworthy, and I did do him a great favour. He told me he had just received the Padre's cassock in the laundry for washing. Would I like to borrow it? What are the chances of that? So the party was Friday night, and the cassock was to be returned on Saturday morning, so I really was being trusted and the consequences of me not getting it back for Sunday service didn't bear thinking about. I spent most of the day making an oversized brass cross and chain, and I found an old hardback book, so I drilled some holes in it and wrote 'Holey Bible' on the front.

After work on Friday afternoon, it was a case of a quick meal and then getting back to the Coastel and changing out of my camouflage gear and into the cassock. As luck would have it, there was no transport available to take us the half-hour walk back to work, so as it was a lovely evening for brisk walking, four of us headed off together. None of the hardcore surfaced road was illuminated in any way, so we just had the moonlight to guide us. And of course with the state of the road, I had to keep lifting the full-length cassock clear of the mud, because I couldn't risk it being returned dirty. On the way, we met a few stragglers meandering back from the camp to their accommodation and their faces were a picture when the new 'Padre', with gold chain and cross round his neck, passed them. Of course everyone knew the real Padre would have been an RAF Officer, so some didn't know whether or not to say hello or salute me, and no-one spoke much, probably because they wouldn't be sure whether to address me as 'Father' or 'Sir'. Others crossed the road because to them it was just weird seeing this cloaked figure emerge from the darkness, and I decided to add to the strange atmosphere by swearing like a trooper as I briskly walked by. A few, who'd consumed a beer or two, uttered a few wisecracks as they passed, or just stared in utter disbelief. If they thought it funny cracking jokes at the Padre, I'd have loved to have seen their faces a few minutes later, because I deliberately walked a good bit in front of a ghost, a witch and a cowboy for maximum effect. I often wonder what would have happened if I'd met the real padre out for his evening stroll. Firstly, I wouldn't have recognised him. I think at that time I'd only ever set eyes on him at the workshop for a repatriation once and he was in RAF Officer's uniform. Secondly, who would have got the biggest shock? One thing's for sure, I know who would have had a hell of a lot of explaining to do!

I decided to stay in character throughout the evening, blessing a few people and tuttering every time I heard a swear word. Lo and behold, I won the competition for best fancy dress, and you won't be surprised to know that the prize was paid in 'trays of beer' currency, and I think that's where I got my Falklands shield and crest. I felt a bit of a con really, considering how much effort some guys made to create an outfit, and I had just picked one off of a clothes hanger.

One thing that the RAF did almost very well, was R&R (Rest and Recuperation). It was traditional, and very much appreciated, that airmen were allowed up to three days away from their workplace for a break, which was only fair considering the length of their tour. You could either organise your own adventure, perhaps to one of the outposts of your choice that the British Forces had on various small islands, or the RAF could organise one for you. Most people who bothered to get involved in the scheme chose places where there was most chance of seeing wildlife. R&R was basically intended to be accommodation somewhere you hadn't visited during your tour, and wasn't related to the type of daily work you typically did.

If you remember, I said in Chapter Two, that, if you befriended someone during the eight days of being on a boat, you were more likely to bond with them rather than work colleagues you spent five months with. Well, someone from our dormitory on the SS *Uganda* was sent to a far-off radar station at Byron Heights (RRH Byron Heights, which stands for Remote Radar Head), almost as far west as was possible on the island of West Falkland. He and I had kept in touch, and I duly arranged with him that I could go and spend two nights there and he would accumulate two days off and show me the best vantage points for whale and sea lion watching. I knew I'd get a lift on any helicopter that ventured that way. Unfortunately, some servicemen can't help themselves, and some nature spotting and appreciation trips turned into seal shooting expeditions, which of course spoiled things for others, so careful monitoring of activities thankfully became more frequent.

Earlier in the chapter, I said that the RAF 'almost' did this well. That's because everyone who wanted did normally get the chance to go, but with the small caveat that this was possible, provided there were no operational reasons to refuse your request. Everything was in place for me to go off on my solo R&R, with time off, travel and accommodation at Byron Heights all booked, and starting four weeks before I was due to leave. However, just before I went, my boss was replaced. Not a problem, surely. Yes, a problem. His replacement, my new boss, had let his aircraft welding qualification fall out of date, so if I was away from the airfield there would be no welding cover, and that was deemed unworkable and an unacceptable risk by the powers that be. I pleaded that surely in the unlikely scenario that I'd be urgently needed, I could be flown back to camp, and after all I was only going for two days, but all the excuses, like the chance of the weather closing in and preventing flights, halted my plan stone dead. Such a pity, and the harsh reality is that sometimes in the Services, No means No. No negotiating, no hard luck tales (very often no common sense), end of story. Of course, I closely monitored the dates that I should have been on R&R and, sure enough, there were no emergency repairs that needed my immediate attention, so I could have easily gone.

Don't you hate it when you think of an alternative, or better idea, long after the event. Thinking about it now, why didn't I see if I could have stopped off on Ascension Island for a couple of days of R&R to wind down when I changed aircraft on the way home. Oh well, I hope someone else learns from this.

# Chapter Six
# – Currencies

There were three types of currency in the Falkland Islands. Namely, the Falklands Pound, the Tray of Beer, and the Four Inch (105 mm) Artillery Shell Case.

The Falklands Pound was exactly as per the British Pound, with identical coins, except that the images on them were much more interesting. The pound coin featured the Falklands coat of arms, while the reverse of the 50p coin had a Warrah, or Antarctic Fox. The 20p coin, again identical to ours in shape, has a sheep, and the picture on the back of a 10p was a South American Sea Lion.

Ironically, one of the smallest coins, the 5p piece, had a black-browed albatross, the biggest bird in the area. The two copper coins featured an upland goose (2p), and Gentoo penguins (1p).

Incidentally, the Ascension Island uses the St Helena Pound, and again, the same value as our Pound, and with identical shaped coins to ours, but with different, and I have to say, very beautiful images on the reverse.

£1 – Sooty (Wideawake) tern, 50p – Turtle (as a coin collector, my favourite), 20p – St Helena Ebony flower, 10p – Dolphin, 5p – Jonathan (a Seychelles giant tortoise, living in Saint Helena, estimated at 191 years old in 2024, making him the world's oldest known living land animal), 2p – Donkey, 1p – Tuna.

I don't know if others did it, but I corresponded with a colleague who was stationed at Ascension Island, and we swapped complete coin sets with each other.

Actually, before I tell you about currencies number two and three, there were actually some mini currencies that you knew to ask for from people in certain departments.

If you did a favour for anyone working in the Medical Centre, the Packet of Strepsils was always a favourite. Everyone had colds and sore throats all the time, so the offer of a packet or two got favours done efficiently. The more Strepsils you brought, the better the attention you received.

I had several dealings with a cook, and when he wanted something doing or repairing, he would come armed with tinned strawberries. Now that was a treat that got him noticed and he would jump the queue for getting my best attention. I knew he was a really switched-on cook because he also brought a tin opener, how thoughtful was that (no ring-pull lids I'm afraid).

Photographers were on the ball. Their bribe was to give you some black and white copies of wildlife or scenic photos (eight inch by six inch I think), they'd taken in the course of their work. Some pictures were just incredible, especially close-ups of wildlife. Also, just to show what an interesting bartering system was in place, a photographer got his ashtray made by me for nothing because he gave me a brand-new Zippo lighter he'd acquired from an Army Division, which I seem to remember may have been infantry. He, in turn, got the lighter from someone in exchange for photos, and so the bartering goes on.

Finally, anyone who was responsible for clothing supplies was always onto a winner. Flying boots were always a very attractive swap, and who would ever turn down extra pairs of thick socks in return for a favour.

The Tray of Beer was another currency, or bartering tool. It cost £3 for 24 tins of beer, probably 330 ml, just like the size of coke cans. I remember servicemen coming into the workshop and looking for a job to be done for themselves, and while cash was always King, the sight of a tray of beer certainly ensured my fullest attention. There was a tradition, when you left the Islands to return home at the end of your posting, that you bought trays of beer for your colleagues' canteen, so I made sure my locker was well stashed ready for the big day, and everyone thought I was very generous, but the beers never cost me a penny.

Thirdly, it was every RAF serviceman's ambition to return to the UK with a brass ashtray (**The Falklands Ashtray**), made from four-inch (105 mm) diameter Shell Cases. These could still be found in the hills and barren areas around Port Stanley. I was in a fortunate position that we had the equipment to make the ashtrays. Most of the conversion from shell case to ashtray was done on a pillar drill and centre lathe, both of which were only found in the Station Workshop. As with a tray of beer, an ashtray cost £3 to make, and of course bribing my hierarchy of bosses by making their ashtrays for no charge, ensured a blind eye was turned to my sideline.

So ashtrays could only be made if you had a shell case, and those lucky enough to find one out in the countryside had to use the Falklands Pound or the Tray of Beer to get their ashtray made. Cash-poor, but asset-rich guys were owners of several shell cases, so they could now use their shell currency to barter for anything. Sometimes aircrew would come into the workshop, say for example from a Hercules C-130, with five shells, wanting five ashtrays made for the crew. Given their rarity, two years after the war, I used to think, 'Where the hell did you get all them?' I never asked questions, it was enough fun watching people when they came into the workshop, with their shell in a paper bag, like an alcoholic tramp hiding his bottle of Buckfast. They'd almost look around worried that people would query where they'd got it, or maybe they feared they'd be mugged, but the big grin on their faces showed they were chuffed because they knew how many others had gone home, never having managed to get hold of one.

Another example of one-upmanship, after establishing that you owned a shell, was to have the oldest date possible, stamped on the base. The majority had 1975–1980 stamped on them, so any earlier was a real bonus. I made my own ashtray, and then kept it locked away until suddenly, someone came in looking for a job lot, e.g. five for a plane's crew. I had a glance over the shells and spotted a 1969 shell in his box. So I got my quick-thinking into action and started a conversation with him to assess if he had any idea what he was dealing with. It became apparent quite quickly that a shell was a shell to him, and dates meant nothing at all, so I laid it on a bit thickly that I was really busy, but promised him a quick turnround, and his ashtrays would be ready next time he landed. So we negotiated that, for a reduction in the fee, I'd swap his 1969 one for the one in my locker, and he was delighted. The crazy fascination for dates meant nothing really to visiting aircrew, only servicemen based at RAF Stanley were constantly comparing and boasting about the year of manufacture. My new possession gave me status, and despite offers of two or threefold the going rate, I declined to sell. A few quid wasn't going to make me part with my prized possession.

Strangely, going back to the date issue, the date is hidden on the bottom of the ashtray, and the centre coin is visible for all to see. Yet, in the Falklands, where you tend to find the most trivial subjects interesting, if you spoke to someone about an ashtray, all the talk was 'What date did you get?' I was amazed at the lack of imagination that the choice of beautiful currency and commemorative coins available for inclusion, wasn't mentioned.

**Hopefully this book won't be published until after my daughter's birthday in August 2024, because she's getting my ashtray for her 50th birthday, almost 40 years to the day from when it was made.** I'd hate to spoil her surprise, so I'll write slowly. Any time she visits me, or when

I move house, she always enquiries as to whether the ashtray is safe, so I reckon she likes it. I think I took the hint when she asked about the 'Family' ashtray before enquiring about me, so she obviously has her eye on her inheritance. Plus, I save money on a birthday present she was going to inherit anyway. Win, win.

I suppose ashtrays can be considered for inclusion into the 'Trench Art' category within antiques and auctionable items. The definition of Trench Art is, 'Any item made by servicemen from any material directly, or any other material, as long as it is connected with armed conflict or it's consequences.' This is further ratified by historian and Trench Art collector Scott Vezeau stating, 'When you take something that once served a military purpose and transform it into either a utilitarian object like an ashtray or a decorative item like a vase, that's Trench Art.'

After viewing countless television shows and listening to even more experts assessing the value of Trench Art, it's fairly obvious that provenance is key. So, below is a copy of my provenance letter with how I've written about, and verified, the origins of my ashtray. The more details and photos giving authenticity to myself and the ashtray, included in the provenance letter, the better.

I've written it in letter form and stored it with the ashtray. One thing to add is that we ensured these ashtrays used to be highly polished before leaving the workshop, and yet the current trend is to have them retained in as close to their natural condition as possible. Loads of guys used to sit for hours on end with a wad of Duraglit, diligently polishing their ashtrays, boasting as to who had the most gleaming brass surface. Nowadays objects, brass especially, hold their value if the patina (natural colouring) is maintained, so mine hasn't been re-polished since 1995.

Provenance is everything.

\* \* \* \* \* \*

105 mm FD: (105 x 326 Light Howitzer separate-loading cased-charged ammunition).

RW 297: (Case design/drawing).

Lot 2: (Manufacturing Batch No).

RLB: (Manufactured by Royal Laboratories Birtley).

1969: (Year of manufacture).

L10A/BN68

288 CY1/69

T8115405 Junior Technician Graham Alan Logie RAF.

Brass 3-slot ashtray with a Falkland Islands 1983, 150th anniversary crown coin pressed into the centre.

This shell was found on the hills across the bay from Port Stanley in the Falkland Islands during my tour of duty May–October 1984. My permanent UK base was RAF Lossiemouth (May 80–Sep 86) at the time.

I formed it into an ashtray in the Station Workshop, which was a 'Rubb' tent type temporary building in August 1984. Most RAF workshop technicians made about 20–30 of these during their 6-month tours of duty between the end of the war in 1982, and the RAF moving to Mount Pleasant Airfield in 1985, so I estimate there are a maximum of 200–250 ashtrays like this in existence, actually made in RAF Stanley. Anyone who wanted one made had to buy their own shells or be lucky enough to find one in the hills and bring them to us to form on a centre-lathe. The standard charge was £3 or a tray of 24 tins of beer for a rush job.

Most ashtrays I made for others had a Falklands 5p or, very rarely, £1 coin pressed in the centre, although I made one for someone using a Falklands Liberation Crown, so I believe this one to be unique. There was a huge case of 'one-upmanship' amongst service personnel with these ashtrays as far as dates stamped on the base were concerned. This one was the oldest I witnessed (1969), with the majority bearing a 1975-1980 date. Obviously, a shell bearing 1982, the year of the 74-day Falklands War (2nd April-14th June) would have been a prized possession but I never witnessed one being brought to us for machining.

Potentially, other artefacts that could be produced from the 105 mm shell cases were Candlestick Holders, Tankards and Bells. I only made one of each of those in my time in the Falklands, with Ashtrays being by far the most popular keepsake. This is the ashtray featured in my book 'THE FALKLANDS ASHTRAY'.

Other facts –

From late 1982 to mid 1985, the RAF had 2 workshop technicians based at RAF Stanley at all times, serving 5-6 month tours. Our trade had been renamed General Technician Workshop (formerly Gen. Fitt WS), a general engineering trade encompassing sheet metal work, welding and machining (centre lathe turning). To be posted there, we were all qualified (or 'Q' annotated in RAF terminology) in aircraft welding. The Navy and Army had no aircraft welders stationed in the Falklands during this time. As well as everyday engineering tasks, we were called upon to weld in situ on 23 Squadron's F4 Phantom aircraft wings as and when air ducts on the trailing and leading edges developed tiny cracks. The welding was done on the aircraft, a job we could do in an hour, but which needed 24 hours if the parts had to be removed from the aircraft, repaired and then replaced. Having previously served for three years (April 77-May 80) at RAF Wattisham, I had the necessary experience of welding Phantom wings.

Sadly and humbly, another task we had to perform in the Falklands, and for which we received no training, or prior warning, was soldering the lids on zinc coffins, a requirement for repatriation of deceased personnel, military and civilian, being flown back to the UK.

We flew to Ascension Island on a British Airways Tristar aircraft, on hire to the RAF, then we were transferred to a ship, SS *Uganda*, by RAF Wessex helicopters for the 7-day sea trip to Port Stanley. I personally had sailed to The Azores, Madeira, Lisbon in Portugal and Vigo in Spain on the SS *Uganda* in 1971 on a school trip when she was a cruise ship. She was subsequently requisitioned in Naples in April 1982, refitted in Gibraltar in only three days, and sent to serve as a hospital ship during the Falklands war and thereafter, from 1983 to 1985 became a stripped-down troop ship sailing from Ascension to Port Stanley.

\* \* \* \* \* \*

Other forms of Trench Art I created in my time at Port Stanley were candlesticks, a tankard and a bell.

I deeply regret not taking more interest in where the handbell ended up. I only ever made one by special request from two or three guys who wanted to take it home for their local pub or club to use for sounding last orders. Goodness knows if it's still in existence, I would love to think so and seeing it 40 years later would be something special. Perhaps this book will jog someone's memory. I imagine it was pretty unique.

As with the bell, I only ever attempted one tankard, made from a single piece of shell, because it was really fiddly to make. Hand cutting the brass sides of the shell to form a handle was time consuming, but then it would only be worthwhile if the handle was then heated, bent and formed successfully. Brass doesn't change colour when heating, and there's a fine line between being nicely heated for bending and melting before your eyes. The one I made worked out well, and the one saving grace was that if the handle had been unsuccessful, there was still enough brass on the shell to make it into an ashtray, so all wasn't lost by any means. I'm sure other tankards may have been attempted by completely soldering a separate handle onto a cut-down shell, but I relished the challenge of making it from a single piece. The bell and tankard were by request only and I never made any more, nor heard of any other engineers attempting them.

Again, I only made one candlestick, which didn't really impress me at the time, but thinking about it now, a pair could be quite sought after. Perhaps there would have been more requests for them if shells had been more readily available.

Being a welder got me some very interesting jobs in the Falklands, and one particular frosty morning, I had to drive to a job which proved interesting to say the least, and also it turned out to be the most frustrating, because not only did I miss out on a trip of a lifetime, I also missed out on the potential to make a different ashtray which would have made me the King of the Ashtrays.

I got a call to drive round to one of the hangars in a remote part of the airfield and was told a Royal Navy Pilot would meet me there. On arrival, I introduced myself and, as he was standing beside a Westland Wasp helicopter (coded EU-421), even I could guess that this was where I was needed.

He explained that his ship, a Leander-class frigate, was about to set sail and head north at the end of her stint with the South Atlantic Protection Force, and would be heading up the eastern coast of South America. He had been ready to take off that morning to rendezvous with the ship and had noticed a crack on the helicopter exhaust pipe. He said it would be frowned upon if the ship had to turn back before it got out of range of the helicopter.

As the naval engineers were on the ship, heading away, and he was on dry land with a poorly helicopter, he was stranded. I had a quick look and reassured him I could fix it pretty rapidly and he'd get on his way. It wasn't really an approved job, no paperwork and no guidelines for how to fix it, unlike normal very strict schedules for aircraft repairs. But, given his enthusiasm for me to get it done quickly, I gathered he wouldn't exactly be flavour of the month if he didn't get this chopper back to his ship.

*Julie's newly acquired ashtray*

*Navy Wasp (HMS Ajax) in for repair*

So, within about 30 minutes, I got it patched up, certainly well enough to get him back, and he assured me they had spares onboard his ship for a more permanent repair to his exhaust cowling.

The poor guy was clock-watching and, as soon as I'd completed the task, he started on about how much he was in my debt and how could he ever repay me. Well, for a start, nobody really knew where I was, and nobody was expecting me back in the workshop anytime soon, so I was delighted not to be rushing back to work. That was a good enough payment for me. The pilot then said that he would get the old boneshaker started up as he had one more delivery to make on the other side of Port Stanley before returning to his ship. I asked him, if he was able to drop me back relatively near here, was there a possibility that I could come for a quick spin with him. He was delighted to oblige, and we both agreed one good turn deserves another.

So, he got her started up, a few pre-flight checks, seatbelt on, headphones on, and off we flew over the bay to the western side of Port Stanley. En route, we got chatting and the subject of brass ashtrays came up. I showed him a photo of one that I'd made, and also a photo of the original shell case.

To say you could have knocked me clean out with a feather after his next comment was no exaggeration. He asked me if the shell in the photo was a four-inch. I told him it was, and he said, 'We often have firing practice when we're at sea, and we have loads of shells lying about. Only thing is ours are bigger than four-inch.' He then went on to say that his shells would probably have been of no use to me.

Oh for goodness' sake, are you kidding, my mind was already in overdrive, where do I start. Firstly, it's certainly not a problem that your shells are bigger than ours, and secondly, they would definitely have been of use to me. The minute he mentioned larger shellcases and plenty of them freely available, I'd already designed them in my head and dreamed of people queuing up to get their hands on one.

I would have had the Islands' most sought-after ashtrays ever if I made it from a different shell case to everyone else's. Everyone wanted something different and, in their eyes, better than anyone else. My heart sank even lower when I asked him what they do with the shell cases. I'll remember his words till my dying day. 'We just throw them over the side; not much use to anyone.'

Worse was to come. He told me that his captain had said that if his ship (HMS *Ajax*) hadn't been sailing away, he'd have flown me out to it for lunch as a thank-you, but as it was heading further away from the island by the minute, the helicopter wouldn't be able to return to RAF Stanley. So I missed out on what would have been a great trip. I imagine it's quite spectacular landing on a moving ship, as my only previous experience was boarding the stationary SS *Uganda*. And, of course, I also missed the chance that, had I got onboard, there could have been the odd dozen or so shellcases lying around, which he said I would have been more than welcome to have taken.

Anyway, I got my two-minute flight over Port Stanley, then two minutes back to the airfield, and he dropped me back at the hangar, a quick handshake and he flew off into the distance.

Certainly a case of so near but yet so far, but the elusive unusual ashtray obviously wasn't meant to be. What a bartering tool that would have been. Being larger, it would also, proportionally, have suited having a crown coin pressed into its centre.

Not only did I have a Royal Navy serviceman to thank for being kind to me, but I had some help from an Army physiotherapist that saved my tour from being cut drastically short after only eight weeks.

I hurt my back and, despite my own best efforts to protect and cure it,

## The Falklands Ashtray   117

I couldn't get rid of the pain near the base of my spine. I tried every pill, lotion, pain relief spray and exercises that I could think of, to no avail. I went to the RAF doctor and we had a good old chat about it and he said it wasn't looking good for me to stay, but he could see I was adamant that a few more days rest could help, so he said the alternatives were for the Army physiotherapist to have a go at giving me stretching exercises to relieve the pain, or I would have to fly home in a few days time if a seat became available on the daily Hercules flight.

I was determined it wasn't going to beat me, so I willingly went to this physio guy for a consultation.

He had a good prod around and, to my surprise, he asked if I was willing to let him have a 'go' at fixing my back. He said it wasn't exactly his area of expertise, which didn't sound terribly professional or confidence-building, and after more back trouble over the next 20 years, I realised he basically carried out a technique that I'd now only expect a trained chiropractor to attempt.

He got me to lie on my back on a treatment bed. He then bent my left leg as he brought it as close to my chest as he could. Then the scary bit – he knelt on my chest, grabbed my upright knee and twisted it sharply 90 degrees to the side. So my chest stayed still and my legs, from my waist down, twisted to the side. I can still hear and feel the noise as my discs appeared to pop, one at a time like the noise of a jacket with press studs being ripped open. There was an eerie silence for 30 seconds, and then he grabbed my wrist and helped me to my feet. I felt tender, but free from pain. A couple of days later I was back working and hillwalking again on my day off.

I had no further contact with the physio, but it sounded like it wasn't exactly his day job to take such drastic action, although, in fairness, he did emphasise it was experimental and the decision was totally mine. I survived without further back pain for the rest of my tour.

Interestingly, after settling back into work on my return to RAF Lossiemouth, I waited till late October and I did what I thought was the sensible thing and made an appointment to see my RAF doctor. I went into his surgery and told him the full story, feeling quite chuffed that I'd got myself the treatment and I just wanted to know if he'd add it to my medical records for future reference. His body language and raised eyebrows told me that this guy wasn't onside with me, and I totally understand and appreciate that there's always been differing opinions between doctors and chiropractors, but his response threw me a bit. He just pointed towards the exit door and said, 'That, young Logie, didn't happen in my eyes and certainly won't be appearing on your records. Good day.' A bit abrupt in my eyes to say the least. He could have been a bit more empathetic and explained his reasoning. I was annoyed that, with his doctor hat on and not his bolshy RAF officer hat, he could also maybe have enquired as to whether my back was actually okay now, since I'd gone to the trouble of making an appointment, but I suppose he enjoyed exercising his authority. A bit of recognition that I worked through the injury and didn't inconvenience anyone with being flown home at short notice on medical grounds, would have been appreciated. Also, if I'd been flown home, someone else would have had to leave their home at extremely short notice to replace me, but again no recognition or thanks.

# Chapter Seven
# – Flights

There were four of us within General Engineering Flight (GEF) who worked closely together in adjoining Rubbs, and all had the same day off every week. Apart from our hillwalking, mentioned in Chapter Three, which we probably did on six of the weeks, we negotiated flights in planes and helicopters on the other days off. There was a general rule of thumb within the airfield, that any flights made by helicopters and transport aircraft that had spare capacity, would welcome servicemen to fly with them, just for the novelty and experience of flying and seeing more of the local area for those who were interested. Luckily, one of our party just seemed to have the knack of knowing who to ask, and he was one of those people who always seemed to be in the right place at exactly the right time when trips became available. It was very much a case of first come, first served, so he was certainly the man in the know.

Flights on a Hercules C-130 were spectacular for all sorts of different reasons. I think we got four flights during our stay, all quite different, and all absolutely unforgettable experiences.

One flight in the C-130 tanker promised to be different to anything we'd witnessed before and we were assured we'd be meeting up with some of the 23 Squadron Phantoms and refuelling them in mid-air. I had visions of sitting somewhere on the plane, and since I hadn't a clue what the inside of a tanker aircraft looked like, thought perhaps we'd be near some windows as the Phantoms approached and maybe get a photo if we were lucky.

I was used to seeing Phantoms from all angles on the ground and in the air in my three years at RAF Wattisham, but the thought of seeing them so close (and for all intents and purposes literally joined on) to another aircraft in the air was very appealing.

As expected, in the inside of the aircraft were blooming big tanks in the middle of the cargo hold, and we took our seats in the hold ready for take off. One thing about the aircrew was that every time we flew, they couldn't have been more patient with us. Nothing was ever any trouble, everything was explained. We all wore headsets and could hear all sorts of conversations between the crew, discussing the flight etc.

The reason for the Hercules tankers being stationed in the Falklands was to provide support for the squadron of Phantoms and to give them maximum time in the air without needing to return to base for fuel.

So, when the Phantoms were heading out for their various sorties, none of which were common knowledge to us, a Hercules was the first plane in the air in the morning and the last to land in the afternoon. Refuelling cover had to be available for all the operational aircraft in case they got into difficulties. The weather was so severe and so changeable that if the last Phantom couldn't land immediately, at least it would have a tanker up in the air with it. And the tanker had a much greater flying time capacity.

Usually, one of us in turn would be invited into the cockpit to experience the view, which was extraordinary compared to sitting in the hold. In calm weather and if there wasn't a lot going on, one of us could stand at the Captain's left shoulder.

The best and most exciting view from a Hercules, is sitting in the spare seat in the middle of the cockpit, behind the two pilots and slightly higher than them. On take off, the experience is spectacular. Some of the time, the plane was touring around, waiting on being called into action by a thirsty Phantom, so the course we flew wasn't written in stone, and if we wanted to see something of interest, we just asked and the pilot would deviate a bit for a better view. Flying past the radar dome on Mount Kent, seeing Port Stanley from the air, studying Goose Green from above, were all fascinating and gave a much better perspective of the layout of the islands.

The pilot and co-pilot decided to have their bit of fun and scare us as we were circling aimlessly, waiting for the first Phantoms to show up. Unbeknown to us, they were selective in what they decided to let us hear through the headsets. As we flew over Mount Kent the first time, they asked us to remove our headsets. We didn't mind because we were fascinated by how low we appeared to be flying in relation to the top of the mountain. Actually, the headsets were removed so that we deliberately didn't hear any communications between aircraft. The closer we got to the summit, the smaller the gap appeared to be. Obviously this was a set-up and we were about to be 'buzzed' when we least expected it. Our crew were in contact with the first two Phantom pilots and, just as we were chatting to each other in the cockpit, and oblivious to anything else in the world, the two Phantoms approached from behind and screamed past below us, between us and the mountain top. The roar, and the buffeting in their slipstream, certainly caught our attention. The communication between ourselves and the other two planes was put on loudspeaker and all you could hear was a couple of eccentric, young Phantom pilots shouting 'Yee-ha' like a pair of Wild West cowboys.

Prior to rendezvousing with the Phantoms, we were given an excellent tour of the hold of the Hercules and the whole refuelling procedure was explained in detail. We were shown the best vantage points for viewing, where potentially the best photos could be taken, and which times we had the freedom to move about the rear of the aircraft, and when to keep well clear of the refuelling hoses.

Through our headsets we heard the first contact with two Phantoms requesting meeting up and refuelling. It was explained to us that they'd make initial visual contact with us by positioning themselves beside our Port (left-hand side) wing. Then our aircrew would roll out the refuelling hose through a slot at the rear of the Hercules. Once fully extended, the first aircraft was invited to position behind us and then gently edge forward to insert its refuelling probe into the basket at the end of our hose. We'd been briefed that this was our opportunity to watch the whole procedure first hand through the hose slot, as we could lie beside the hose and get a bird's eye view. The only safety procedure we had to be aware of (and no, we couldn't fall out of the slot, as it was too small for that) was that if for any reason the Phantom, once connected up, pushed our hose too quickly, it would recoil back onto the drum inside the Hercules. As the hose was very heavy and rigid, it could give us a fair whack on the side of our body as we laid beside it. So, should such an occurrence happen, and it would be quick, the aircrew onboard with us would give our foot a quick kick and we knew to roll clear of the hose.

I don't think there's words (that's awkward when I'm supposed to be writing a book) to describe just how thrilling it was to be so close to another aircraft in mid-air and travelling at speed, and witness how quick and efficient the whole process was. I honestly felt like I could reach out and tap the windscreen of the Phantom. It was mind-blowing.

As soon as the transfer of fuel was complete, the Phantom disconnected and moved across to our other wingtip on the Starboard side and maintained that position until his partner approached us for his top-up. The aircrew were very helpful and let each one of us in turn lie beside the hose for, as the photo shows, the best views of the operation.

As you'll remember, I spoke previously about the different 'currencies' used in the Falklands. Well, the Phantom pilots were pretty clued up on that.

The Falklands Ashtray 123

*Phantom refuelling*

*Phantom on starboard wing after refuelling*

If, perchance, when approaching the refuelling hose behind the Hercules, the Phantom pilot was overly enthusiastic and rammed the tapered 'basket' on the end of the hose, and inadvertently damaged the basket by piercing the side, there was a forfeit to pay. When the Hercules landed, the ground crew would have to replace the basket of their aircraft, which was broken by the crew of a different aircraft. So, the forfeit or punishment charged to the Phantom pilot was to pay for his error. The currency payable, and no invoices or receipts were exchanged, was trays of beer. Preferably several trays of beer. Needless to say the Phantom pilots we observed connected impeccably first time, both aircraft. I suppose on nearly every flight at that time there were some airmen on their first and only ever flight in a tanker aircraft, so the sight of a few cameras trained on them gave them that little incentive not to mess up.

Needless to say, time on such an interesting trip flew by (pun absolutely intended) and it seemed like no time at all before we got confirmation that the last Phantom on the current sortie had landed and there was no further need for the Hercules to remain airborne. It was actually quite disappointing to be returning to the airfield, and I can't emphasise enough our appreciation for the crew's patience, but we were excited to see how our photos were going to turn out. It was still the age of 35 mm film and waiting a few days to develop them.

One memorable Hercules C-130 flight that we managed to get a ride with was a mail drop to South Georgia. This time not in a tanker but a regular cargo plane. It was arranged to do a mail drop at Grytviken on King Edward Cove, one of the best harbours and shelters in it's day, where a disused whaling station stands. The cove is on the northerly coast of the island, and all we were told before take-off was that the drop was to be in the sea and picked up by a survey team working in the area.

South Georgia is over 800 miles east of the Falkland Islands, so we were prepared for a decent length of flight. We'd witnessed various mail and package drops at remote parts of the Falklands on previous helicopter flights we'd been on, and they simply opened a door and chucked the package out at low level. This, however, was to turn out to be a more spectacular and memorable sight.

So we took off mid-morning and headed east. We had packed lunches with us, again the Mess was very supportive of servicemen using their initiative and getting out and about on their days off. Between poor visibility and empty seas, there wasn't an awful lot to look at on the way. Aircrew, as it turned out, were equally as interested to hear about our jobs and what we were doing in the Falklands, just as much as being onboard a flight interested us.

Time flew by as we reached and then followed the northern coast of South Georgia, looking at some of the sights. There had been several settlements and whaling stations over the years in South Georgia, but most looked to be in a pretty sorry state now. We reached the point for our task for the day and, noticeably, no-one was very forthcoming with any details of how the drop would be done. This, we found out, was to give us maximum effect of the quite spectacular technique they adopted.

Firstly, we were all told to sit down on the seats along the edges of the hold and fasten our seat belts. We had an idea the drop was imminent because we had slowed down and were now flying lower. The next move surprised us because they then opened the rear ramp/door of the aircraft which is basically the entire back of the plane. Then, the crew hung a cargo net across the whole doorway. The noise was now considerable as we were hearing the four engines outside us, and it got an awful lot colder.

After everything was in place, we prepared for the best free roller coaster of a ride, as it was explained to us that all four of us were now going to lay on the net. Well, it took a bit of guts to lay on it with only the

*Chinook over Moody Brook*

*Typical South Georgia view*

net between us and the freezing South Atlantic Ocean below. It was in the days before mobile phones were part of our lives but the holes in the net were certainly small enough for us not to fall through, and big enough to photograph through, while being mindful that they were also big enough to drop my antiquated camera through, so great care was taken.

We could only see the sea out the back door because we were approaching land, flying directly towards the cove and, once a crew member got the signal, the pilot lifted the aircraft's nose, the engines roared louder and we started climbing steeply. The package was tossed out of the back of the plane and, because of the steep angle of climb, we were now staring directly down to the sea. It was absolutely breathtaking and something we never expected. The rapid climb showed just how versatile the Hercules was and we were high up and heading away before we could see how the pickup went.

Now for a two-hour flight back to RAF Stanley, but we had some work to do, or rather the aircrew had, on the way back. South Georgia is on a notorious iceberg route, so any really large ones were to be plotted and reported. We didn't see anything really major, although every iceberg is spectacular in its own way, and I suppose that at the height we were flying, it would be very difficult to appreciate the real size of the iceberg. And, of course, icebergs, by their nature, can be enormous under the water line, so we only witnessed a fraction of their mass. However, the sea looked more interesting than I'd ever seen it. I'd never been so far south in my life and heavy hail and snow showers calmed the sea and made it look incredibly dark against the white snowfalls.

Interestingly, though, icebergs were a minor distraction, because the real reason we flew a meandering path on the way home was to check up on any boats in our vicinity . From the remoteness of a boat in this area, it must be very comforting to see a friendly plane (as you'll read, we may not have been considered quite so 'friendly' to some) fly low overhead. Just knowing someone else was in the area must have been reassuring, providing of course, that you were sailing legitimately, and going about your day's work. There were some very genuine boats navigating their way in the South Atlantic Ocean and carrying their vital cargoes between continents. By this time, we were invited into the cockpit and got a really good view of what our crew were looking for. We made contact with a couple of ships. Their crews were only too happy to chat and wished us well as we flew overhead.

Not all boats were as welcoming or as delighted to see us. On seeing any that didn't look like genuine deep-sea trawlers, we'd head in their direction and fly low and slow overhead. Just to make sure that no-one was in any doubt that we'd seen them, we'd make two or three passes from different directions. This also gave our crew more chances to photograph from varied angles. Most didn't make contact, or if they did, they suddenly remembered that they spoke very limited English. The concerning thing about 50 per cent of them was that they had more ariels than fishing nets or gear on their decks. I could only imagine that below deck there were more radio operators than fish processors. The closer we got to the Falklands, the more 'fishing' boats we encountered, so it was just a case of photographing them, and I'm sure that when we landed our crew would be debriefed and would pass on their sightings. Another obvious clue as to these boats being up to no good, was the lack of flags identifying their country of origin, as well as a lack of country or city of registration being displayed.

Again, like the tanker crew, our hosts for the day couldn't have been more accommodating, so we showed our appreciation with the customary currency of a tray of beer, or a promise to make their ashtrays free of charge if they got hold of any shells.

One day, my colleagues surpassed themselves and organised another helicopter trip, but this time in a Chinook. Come to think of it, these guys never went missing during working hours in the Rubb next door to my workshop, they never seemed to wander off, and I was never aware of them befriending servicemen from different parts of the camp, but yet they were always first to hear about availability of spaces on flights and always sounded out good trips. I wonder how they did it. I can only think that, as tradesmen working on aircraft ground support equipment, they kept their ears and eyes open when delivering equipment to the aircraft.

None of us knew what to expect this time, and it was certainly an ambition of mine to fly in a Chinook. The RAF Chinook was on a test flight after some repairs, so they were only too happy to offer a few seats.

Unlike the routine flights with Bristows, where we jumped in and out the aircraft like a glorified taxi, this time we got a bit of a safety briefing and were told not to expect any landings anywhere, but there could be a few different tests of the aircraft, so remain seated in case of unexpected sharp climbs or left and right turns.

So we duly entered through the rear ramp, a pretty impressive start, got settled in and were immediately impressed with the noise and vibration as the aircraft started up. Take off was a quick vertical climb, then the nose dropped and off we went at speed. This was so different, the noise, the power, and soon we'd crossed the harbour and passed alongside Windy Ridge, a route we all recognised from our hillwalking excursions.

It was nice to see and feel what it was like speeding along at reasonably low level, because we'd experienced seeing and hearing Chinooks many times from the ground, as we walked alongside Moody Brook and could imagine exactly what it would be like for anyone walking below us.

Then, we had headsets on by the way, we heard the pilot's voice with an announcement we didn't really expect or want to hear. One of the components they were testing was still faulty and the only course of action was to return to the airfield and hand the aircraft back to the ground crew.

Again, something new to us was the pilot apologising profusely to us, the guests. He said they'd wanted us to enjoy the trial as it usually meant

*Lady Elizabeth at low tide*

*Onboard Lady Elizabeth*

they could throw her about a bit to test everything. So seat belts on and we headed back to base, but just before we landed the pilot radioed that he would show us a party piece unique to Chinooks to make up for the disappointment of the unexpectedly short flight. I was already tickled pink at having achieved a bit of an ambition by flying in a Chinook, but thought this was an extra bonus. Approaching the runway, the rear ramp suddenly lowered and we flew the entire length of the runway literally 10 or 20 feet off the ground. It was quite bizarre to see the airfield from this unusual angle. Then, and this was the party piece, the rear wheels touched down at the end of the runway leaving the nose of the aircraft up in the air. We then reversed the entire length of the runway in that position, then further reversed into another side plinth. What a clever piece of skill (was it airmanship or driving?) and fascinating to be part of, but as with the help and kindness we'd experienced from other flights, it showed the camaraderie between different trades and departments within RAF Stanley.

On one particular day off, instead of flying or walking, we decided that, since the weather was nice by Falklands standards, and there was an extremely low tide, we would have a real close up look at one of the islands' most iconic sights, the wreck of the *Lady Elizabeth*.

She is described as one of the best-preserved wrecks on the Falklands. I'd go further and say she's without doubt the most impressive wreck I've ever seen in my life. The *Lady Elizabeth* lies in Whalebone Cove, which is basically the most eastern point of Stanley Harbour. We passed her every day, to and from work, so getting a closer look was appealing.

The nautically uneducated amongst us, myself included, would refer to her as a schooner or sailing ship but her official classification is actually a three-masted Barque.

I don't suppose I'll have an opportunity like it again to go up to a,

*Lady Elizabeth bowsprit*

*Lady Elizabeth at sunset (competition winning photo)*

at that time, 105-year-old ship, and touch the hull that braved and was pounded by the mountainous seas of the South Atlantic for 33 years.

The *Lady Elizabeth* had got into difficulties sailing round Cape Horn in 1912, losing her deck cargo and four sailors. She limped towards Port Stanley and unbelievably hit Uranae Rock, 15 miles from Port Stanley, and was holed, on her way towards shelter. She was towed into Stanley Harbour, declared unseaworthy and became a floating coal and wood storage facility. In 1936, during a fierce storm, she broke free of her moorings and washed up on the beach in Whalebone Cove, exactly where she is to this day.

There were no restrictions at all placed on visiting the wreck, and as she's sitting embedded on sand, it's easy to walk up to her at really low tides. Now I say no restrictions, but there was strong advice from the Service Hierarchy that climbing aboard and wandering her rotting, wooden decks was dangerous to say the least. It would have been frowned upon if anyone got hurt and lost time at work through recklessly ignoring the advice. So that's good enough for me – we duly clambered aboard and, as you can see from my photos, she was truly spectacular.

I won a photo competition on the Falkland Islands with my picture of the Lady Elizabeth at sunset. I can't even begin to remember what the prize was, but I'm sure it would have been some sort of Falkland Islands memorabilia, an ornament, or dare I say it, another tray of beer. I was by no means an accomplished photographer, and my camera would have been cheap and very amateurish, but to my astonishment, I won. Given the standard of competition, including some very serious amateur photographers with all their fancy cameras with obscenely long lenses, I was very proud of myself. In fact 'smug' might have described me better.

# Chapter Eight
# – The Trailer

The biggest project, adventure and experience all rolled into one was meeting Mark Harrisson, a helicopter pilot with Bristows. Mark flew a Sikorsky S-61 helicopter, similar to RAF Sea Kings, one of three on hire from Bristows to the Ministry of Defence. Such red, white and blue helicopters were a far more familiar sight in the skies over Aberdeen, ferrying oil workers to and from their rigs in the North Sea. By good fortune, someone I trusted to proof read this book, recognised Mark's name and knew someone who knew someone, and Mark and I are now back in touch after 40 years which alone makes this all worthwhile.

The helicopters were the workhorses of the day, routinely flying servicemen or equipment between Port Stanley and the many outposts and islands around us. Goose Green was a regular calling point, but they'd go as far as Fox Bay and Lively Island in the South, and West Point in the western extremity of West Falkland.

As mentioned before in Chapter Seven, any spare capacity onboard any routine or non-emergency flights were always made available to anyone interested in flying or in seeing more of the islands. Mark kept us up to speed with any forthcoming flights that he was piloting, and it was worth trying to wangle time off or, more extremely, change your day off if a decent trip was planned.

One trip that I'm glad we got the opportunity to go on was predominantly a penguin spotting trip to Strike Off Point, about 15 miles north-east of Port Stanley, which has a very accessible penguin colony.

The trip was actually a planned excursion by the RAF as a sort of respite nature watch afternoon, to get up and close to local wildlife in supervised controlled conditions. It was important that people didn't just wander off and do their own thing, mainly because of uncharted minefields, but also to protect wildlife from the trauma of intruders.

There were spare seats, so we actually got some free time off for an interesting afternoon. I think we persuaded our bosses it was an educational trip, and we were supporting the authorities by attending. The penguin colony was the main focus, so we had someone who was a bit of an authority on wildlife with us to explain how to see them, how not to frighten them, and where we were and weren't allowed to go.

I was expecting lots of beaches because, typically, penguin colonies are often photographed waddling up from the sea and over a sandy beach, but the terrain was quite different. There was a beach and we landed in long grassy land on a hillside about two hundred yards above it. We were given quite a free rein to have a recce around, being told not to venture too far from the helicopter, and to return immediately if we got a call that the wildlife wasn't enjoying our presence. The rules were simple – don't endanger or upset any wildlife or the trip would be immediately ended. This was a great chance to see wildlife, especially the penguins, at really close quarters, so it made sense to respect the colony and to proceed slowly and quietly.

With us all wearing our standard camouflage gear, and being a couple of hundred yards up a hill, we thought we'd be creeping slowly down towards the beach unnoticed and photographing the penguins waddling and swimming at the water's edge. So we walked and crept slowly along the hillside, reassured by the fact that we were told there were definitely penguins in the area, but also wondering had they just returned to the sea? Had the helicopter scared them off? Or were they just hiding from us?

Moments later, we got the biggest surprise of the afternoon, when we heard this honking, squawking, unmistakable noise of a large colony of penguins. The only problem was, they weren't below us on the beach waiting to pose for photographs, they were behind us, even further up the hill than we were, so we were now in their way and, as far as they were concerned, they were going in a straight line to the shore and to hell with anyone or anything in their path. Because we were crouched low, they didn't seem to think we were a problem on their stampede to the sea. Everyone was very responsible though and quickly sprinted off to the side, allowing the mass to pass by reasonably close to us. Apparently, although groups of penguins are mostly referred to as Colonies, a number of penguins walking is also known as a Waddle, which seemed very apt as we watched them pick up speed.

It certainly wasn't the environment I'd expected to see my first close up penguins in, and they seemed very adept at negotiating the hillside, allowing us to take a few unexpectedly good photos. After they passed, the responsible thing to do was wait till they'd reached the sea before starting up the helicopter and making our exit.

Another trip that Mark ensured we could be on was a delivery of goods to Goose Green. Quite simple and routine even for that part of the world you may think, but we had good reason as he was going to show us his mysterious 'little project' that he wanted myself and my three walking colleagues to be part of.

My mind was curious, did he want to photograph something, did he want our advice, although I can't think why, or did he just think we would be in awe of the place, considering its wide television coverage two years previously.

I thought he'd keep us guessing, in fact my other three colleagues were the ones who first befriended Mark, so I thought maybe they were in on this great mystery and it was just me who was travelling blind that day. As soon as we landed and I was told the reason for my presence, I could quite easily have been knocked over with a proverbial feather. I think my initial reaction was, 'Are you serious, how in the name of creation are we going to get away with this. In fact, is this even legal.'

The task, even when said quickly, seemed impossible. All he wanted to do was to take an abandoned Argentinian aircraft back to the UK and, as a welder, could I please make a trailer to get it to a ship.

Totally unofficially, of course, no paperwork, nothing to do with the RAF, completed in our own time, oh, and could you please make it 33 feet long (including 16 feet towbar), 8 feet wide, 8 feet high, and with two axles. The reason I thought the others were way ahead of me in this plan, was that I started blurting out questions like, 'Where will we get the material?' 'How on earth are we going to find two axles and wheels capable of carrying a damn plane?' And, 'Where on earth are we going to build it?'

The others, my devious colleagues, were quick, too quick, to answer my three questions. 'There's all the materials we need along with twin axles from a lorry in the scrap compound along the road from the workshop. And the workshop floor space is over 60 feet long.' So it looks like this is a done deal, I'll do all the welding, they'll do all the labouring and it would appear that every evening for the next month is going to be taken up.

So, now that I'm here in Goose Green, and obviously the plane is here, it made sense to go and see the scale of this project that we seem to be committed to. Sitting on a gentle slope on a hillside on the outskirts of the village was Alpha-517, an Argentinian FMA IA-58 Pucará aircraft. Her nickname 'GARRA GLOBU' stencilled in faded black ink on her green/khaki camouflage, and just visible on the port side of her nosecone.

The history of it was that the Argentinian Air Force (Fuerza Aérea Argentina FAA) landed it at the airfield in Port Stanley and then

*Mark with A-517 at Goose Green*

*Bristow's helicopter on hillside at Strike Off Point*

subsequently flew it to Goose Green, two days before the beginning of the war. Then, when it was needed to fly again to avoid it from being attacked by British Harrier jets, the nosewheel got stuck in soft ground as it was taxiing, and the front undercarriage collapsed. It never flew again and was written off, but eventually the undercarriage was hastily repaired enough for her to be manhandled to another area, away from the Goose Green landing strip, to act as a decoy to entice British Harrier jets in an attempt by Argentinian Forces to shoot them down.

After the war, the aircraft was robbed by bounty hunters of its cockpit dials and switches etc., and a few panels with roundels and Attack Group 3 badges were cut away and removed. I was never quite sure if the metal outer panels were removed by trophy hunters, aircraft enthusiasts, or entrepreneurs out to make a quick buck, or just aggrieved locals who didn't want Argentinian livery staring them in the face every time they passed it. Some people, probably through resentment because it was Argentinian, used it as a shooting target. Then, rather than move it, at the end of hostilities the British Ministry of Defence gifted the rather bare airframe to the Goose Green community. I'm not sure why it was assumed that the community would want this sorry looking relic as some sort of souvenir or exhibit, but as it happens, it was quickly discounted as being of any sort of sentimental value. Perhaps gifting money to rebuild the community and promising to scrap this eyesore would have been received graciously by the community, but offering them a relic belonging to a country who'd just invaded them seems a tad insensitive. Still I suppose, the MoD's 'gift' could turn out to be Mark's gain.

Mark managed to buy the Pucará from the community who had assured him they didn't really want this rusting, stark reminder of the hostilities on their doorstep and he befriended them to the extent that many of the original parts started finding their way out of homes and sheds and thankfully back to the plane.

And so began his quest to transport it home to the UK.

I had to admire his enthusiasm as transporting it anywhere within the UK would have been hard enough, but to arrange to move the plane across rugged terrain to the shore, load it on a boat and then eventually transport it eight thousand miles by sea must have taken endless hours of planning and negotiation.

Apparently, the aircraft is very simply but robustly built to suit field conditions, and the wings can be relatively easily removed, so the trailer he required had to have upright metal posts along each side. The design meant the detached wings could be laid along the length of the floor of the trailer, then webbing straps were to be strung across the uprights and the fuselage would then lay on the straps like a hammock.

Using a borrowed tractor or Unimog, the trailer was intended to be dragged across the mixture of rough terrain and tracks, towards the nearest pier, where it could be put on MV *Monsunen* to take it to Port Stanley, and then it would be transferred to a sea-going ship.

That was the plan. A few minutes ago I was flabbergasted that I was expected to magically create a huge trailer out of nothing, and now I'm rather glad that I now only had to build a trailer, rather than organise such an epic trip. I actually left the Falklands days after we finished making the trailer, so I never witnessed any of the onward journey. However, I have recently managed to catch up with the resulting next 40 years of A-517's life.

The aircraft did in fact make it to the UK in three shipping containers. Strangely and intriguingly, it acquired British Civil Aviation Authority registration in record time, before, as it happens, it even left the Falklands, and was then known as G-BLRP. This registration was revoked in 1995. There are five other known 'British Pucarás' (A-515, A-522, A-528, A-533 and A-549 are in varying states of repair, displayed in museums across England) but the whereabouts of A-517 was a great mystery. Over the years, its location was never known, although it did appear on paper records as having been sold on at least once. Finally, it's location, still unfortunately in containers, is now verified as being in

Forest City in North Carolina, owned by South African born Rodney Butterfield, an automotive design engineer. To say the aircraft is in a worse than sorry state is no exaggeration, and perhaps restoration to a static display condition is probably the best that can be hoped for. Unlike Mark's dream of it being a flying exhibit by the early 1990s, hoping to grace British Air Displays as the only serviceable flying Pucará in the UK. I used to look out for A-517 at airshows and in aviation magazines without success. Now I realise why.

I don't think I even had time to realise how cold it was on that Goose Green hillside, and I don't remember trying to look around at the bleak surroundings, which is what I wanted to experience. This was my only visit to Goose Green, and I really wish I'd taken more time to see some infamous landmarks and tried to get my bearings so that next time I hear about the area, I could envisage what was being talked about. I was now just the proud owner of a single foolscap (forerunner to A4) sheet of paper with some crazy-sized dimensions drawn on it, and the promise of earning a few quid in return for building a rather large trailer.

So, this led to a lengthy period of cramming in trailer building into every spare minute we had. We were already working twelve-hour days, so why not exhaust ourselves even more. Credit where credit's due, the other three did every single bit of labouring and I really only had to weld what they put in front of me. I used to refer to them as the Three Wise Men for all the flights and hillwalking they used to organise for me, but at that point, they were temporarily named Dumb, Dumber and Even Dumber Still, as they schemed up this unlikely project. They, in turn used to say they were my 'agents', but I assured them I didn't want any more contracts negotiated on my behalf, thank you.

Sure enough there was a scrap compound just along the road from the workshop and, handily, it was right at the roadside. Compound usually means there's a big fence all around, but this just had an enormous ditch. Secondly, there were ample heavy H-beams and lengths of angle iron, and, would you believe it, there were two lorry vehicle axles, complete with wheels, fastened to guess what – a lorry. The metal and axles could only be retrieved by stretching a HIAB across the ditch, and who was the only person they knew that had an HGV and HIAB licence? Me. So now I see where I'm fitting into all this. No-one really knew who was in charge of the scrap metal compound, or how the piles of metal got there, or whether it was okay just to help yourself. So we worked on the basis of Finders, Keepers as long as no-one told us any differently. Luckily, I think that everyone who saw us stealing (sorry, recycling) metal was probably as ignorant as us, and they more than likely assumed we had full permission and were working in 'our' compound.

Remember all this was done without our bosses' knowledge. Hiding an ashtray, perhaps, was reasonable, but a 33-feet-long trailer, over 8 feet high, now that was deviousness at a whole new level, especially as, for the first few evenings, it didn't have any wheels on it, so it was hoisted into the workshop and dragged out with the lorry. I remember signing out the lorry really early one morning and giving a totally fictitious reason for needing it, then blocking the road for nearly an hour to retrieve bits from the scrap pile. When lifting anything with a HIAB, or any other lifting device, it's important to know the weight of it. So, again, one morning, really early before our bosses came to work, I signed out a lorry with HIAB to turn over the trailer which up to now had been welded in the upside-down position, with axles and wheels now attached. We hadn't a clue whether it was within the safe working capacity, but anyway we got it up onto its side. I keep saying 'we' because if this went wrong, I wasn't in the mood for taking all the blame. Then, trying to lower it, I was petrified it would go part of the way, then jolt as it toppled over. This thing could have weighed a few tons. The pessimist in me was already picturing the lorry toppling over beside it because the HIAB wasn't made for heavy lifts, and my brain was pondering excuses as to why the road could have been blocked and a lorry damaged. My fears were unfounded, the mission was completed successfully, so I could definitely breath again, and then I strutted around looking as though I was in full control of the situation.

But we did it, we completed the trailer, and very proud we were too, just before my time in the Falklands was up and I had to leave the others who had a few more days left to do on the Islands. So they handed over the trailer to its new owner and I never found out how much of the aircraft removal operation they witnessed. Suffice to say it must have been successful because the Pucará made it back to the UK, stuffed inside containers, with, as it happens, assorted parts of other random aircraft including a Bell UH-1 helicopter (nicknamed Huey because it was launched originally as an HU-1, but redesignated to UH-1 in 1962), before ending up in the States.

And so, in early October 1984, the planning for my return trip to the UK started. Traditionally, we had an evening of beers in our canteen after work, so my stash of trays of beer went to very good use. My replacement hadn't quite arrived, so I was unable to pass on helpful tips about some of the less common jobs we were expected to do (soldering coffins springs to mind). Unfortunately, I missed out on ending the tour with another 'trip of a lifetime' opportunity. A Royal Navy destroyer was sailing home at roughly the same time, and they offered three RAF personnel the chance to work their passage and join the ship for a five-week trip home via stopovers in the Caribbean and Florida. I couldn't afford my first foreign holiday until 1987, so the mention of Florida just seemed a world away from what I was used to. This was too much for some people on top of an already arduous six months away from home, but when

*Turning the trailer over (myself in lorry)*

*Completed trailer*

the RAF opened up the availability to anyone leaving within a certain timespan, I thought I'd have a good chance, assuming I'd be one of very few applicants. Usually something like this would be the talk of the camp, or at very least the main subject of conversation in the works canteen or the Mess, but strangely no-one mentioned it so I got to thinking that maybe very few people even knew about it. But it was not to be when the names were drawn out of the hat, I was name number five, so very little chance of two people dropping out in a very short time. It was to be a much quicker set of flights home for me.

The day came and, believe it or not, it was tinged in a bit of sadness, in between relief and sense of achievement. Myself, my predecessors and no doubt, my successors, really made the workshop a very efficient and enjoyable workplace and again, apart from the pressures of being away from home, I was going to miss the friends and lifestyle we'd become very used to. We'd been made very aware that work was progressing at Mount Pleasant, but it didn't really sink in that RAF Stanley was only going to be in existence for less than four years and I'd been lucky enough to have been part of it. This time there was to be no long, dreary sailing on the SS *Uganda* or even the MV *Keren*. The first flight I took to Ascension Island was by the Hercules C-130 Airbridge.

The jokers and scaremongers in the RAF camp couldn't resist one last tease of everyone going home, so they started rumours that anyone 'smuggling' Falklands currency, or brass shell case ashtrays out of the country would have them confiscated. They started to sound convincing as they claimed, 'How do you think the Customs guys get their ashtrays?'

But on the day it was really efficient. Minimal paperwork and we seemed to waltz straight through the terminal building and onto the aircraft. I often wondered what it was like for anyone involved in dispatching the aircraft and watching happy faces going home virtually every day for six months. Onboard it was now hours and hours of sitting squashed along both sides of the aircraft, which didn't make for a pleasant flight, and sleep was practically impossible with the noise and vibration. Funnily enough, all the Hercules flights we'd had while based in the Falklands seemed like an adventure, but now this was a long journey home that everyone wanted to be uneventful and quick. Ascension Island was a much more welcoming sight this time for a quick stopover and change to a different aircraft. The heat was more than welcome, and no doubt we wouldn't have objected to a couple of days' stopover, but there were too many of us and everyone just wanted to get home.

Delays were minimal at Ascension, no checking notice boards for flight times. The onward-bound plane was sitting waiting for us, and in no time we were boarding an RAF VC-10 aircraft. This was now luxury after the noise and vibration inside the Hercules. The VC-10 was quite strange to get used to if it was your first flight in one, as all the seats faced backwards. One reason that this wasn't a problem for me, though, was that, at the window seat on my side of the aircraft, my lasting vision of Ascension Island was of tearing down the runway, then getting a good view of the endless, brown, volcanic ash landscape as we ascended. We then rose through some thick cloud and then, magically, the summit of Green Mountain appeared, towering 895 metres above sea level, and suddenly everything was lush and green. It was almost like a picture in a children's book with a sort of fairytale land high above the rest of the island. All too soon, though, it disappeared from view and we were truly UK bound.

After a real sleep, we descended into RAF Brize Norton on a typically rainy October afternoon and already the Falkland Islands were a bit of a distant memory, and as I said at the beginning, viewing the continuing miners' strike on a TV screen within minutes of entering Arrivals, brought it home that the excursion was well and truly over and it was back to reality.

After two fairly arduous flights back-to-back, I was given a room at Brize Norton for the night, then unceremoniously dropped off at Heathrow the next day. The rest of the journey home was relatively uneventful. The only minor hiccup could have been that, after being bussed to Heathrow,

I went to the flight desk with a travel warrant for a specific flight taking off in over 20 hours' time. I asked the clerk if she could change it to an earlier flight because there was a flight to Glasgow in less than two hours' time. She said she couldn't possibly alter an official Air Force warrant, which disappointed me. But then she said, 'But of course if you were to do it, not a problem.' I stopped caring about whether warrants should or shouldn't be tampered with. Out came my pen and now the warrant said, 'Any available flight.' The RAF weren't particularly flexible when it came to trusting us with warrants, tickets, expenses, etc., so I thought, 'To hell with them, surely after what I've done for them, a little alteration on a travel warrant isn't going to hurt anyone.'

From Heathrow it was a Trident 3 jet aircraft to Glasgow, then another wait for the last leg in a Viscount turboprop to Aberdeen. I just laughed to myself that on each flight it seemed to be that the further North I travelled, the more basic the aircraft. Just as well I wasn't going any further.

Train to Elgin, taxi to the house and, guess what? Work tomorrow.

Not exactly a tickertape welcome, but I'm sure everyone was glad to see me. I was now facing a million questions from servicemen, family and neighbours who never got the chance to experience the Falklands, but I'm glad that I could pass on invaluable guidance to anyone who did head out there after me. And the opportunity to write a book 40 years later, who'd have guessed that?!

# AUTHOR BIO

Aberdeen-born Graham Logie was raised on the island of Islay off Scotland's south-west coast. His early working life was spent as a welder in the Royal Air Force from 1974–86.

In May 1984 he got the 'opportunity' to spend five months at RAF Stanley in the Falkland Islands.

Now retired and living near Bath in Somerset, Graham took to writing, and his first book, *Give Her Six*, recorded his early years living on an island, while this, his second book, relates stories and shares personal photographs of what life was like in this temporary RAF camp. Stories and photos which Graham feels should be recorded for future generations because it was like no other camp.

Graham's 'conversational' style of writing is very much his own unedited words, and his natural humour shows through in every chapter.